Jesus Christ
Our
Approach
Offering

David Bergey

JESUS CHRIST
OUR APPROACH OFFERING

Copyright © 2004 by David Bergey
Second Edition
All Rights Reserved

No part of this book may be reproduced, stored in a retrieval system, or transmitted, in any form or by any means: electronic, mechanical, photocopy, recording, or any other, except for brief quotes in printed reviews, without permission of the author.

ISBN 1-59196-565-9

Printed in the U. S. A.

*Dedicated to
Jim Stutz*

Acknowledgments

This book is dedicated to Rev. Jim Stutz (1950-2002). When I first started my studies on Old Testament sacrifices in 1998, Jim provided knowledgeable assistance and godly encouragement. No doubt, this work would have been better caliber had his continued assistance been available.

Karen Heckler was my main editor. Without her invaluable help, this book would have been published—just not in this decade. She edited my truly rough drafts into something readable.

In producing this work I have incurred a multitude of debts. In reviewing, encouraging and editing, Doug Seed, Dan and Randi Moran, Bob Lindfelt, Bob Falk, Bob Lambert and my dad, Chester Bergey, pitched in. Lynn Morrison and Jorge Dieppa were of much assistance in the minutia of the final edits. These have saved me from many errors, great and small, as well as aided in readability and clarity. Nevertheless, they cannot take the blame for mistakes; the final contents are my sole responsibility.

Thanks to my wife, Mary, for her cheerful patience and support while I robbed time from her and our children and my business to produce this work.

I am most thankful to God for the countless times He has thrilled and melted my heart at the ineffable greatness of the Scriptures.

Contents

Acknowledgments *i*

Preface 1

Chapter 1: Introduction: Jesus Christ, 3
The Way into God's Presence
    Access is Influence
    Why Study Old Testament Sacrifices?

Chapter 2: Leviticus: Approaching God with an 20
Approach Offering
    The Two Functions of the Five Offerings of Leviticus 1-7
    Approaching God with an Approach Offering
    The Approach, *Qarab*, Emphasized by the Figure of Speech,
        Polyptoton

Chapter 3: Approaching God in Prayer 37
    Qarab, To Approach
    Qatar, To Burn as Incense
    Incense Represents Prayer
    Approaching God in Prayer in the New Testament

Chapter 4: Jesus Christ: Our Approach Offering 53
    Prosagōgē, Access by an Intermediary
    Brought Near
    Jesus Christ, Our Approach Offering in Romans and Hebrews
    Theme of Hebrews: Approaching God
    Jesus Christ as Intercessor in Romans and High Priest in
        Hebrews
    Believing to Approach God in Romans and Hebrews
    "I am the Door"
    "I am the Way"

Chapter 5: The Veil Rent 77
    Our Entry through the Veil
    The Salt Covenant

Chapter 6: Our Right of Boldness in Approach 92

Our Accomplished Boldness
   Fallen Man's Approach
   Our Approach to God by the Spirit
   Our *Parrhēsia* by the Spirit in I John
   Utilizing Our Boldness: Approaching with Full Assurance

Chapter 7: Without Blemish Before Him in Love   118
   Without Blemish in Leviticus
   Our Cleansing in Jesus Christ

Chapter 8: Holy Before Him in Love   133
   Holiness Defined Holiness under the Law
   "The Nadab and Abihu Incident"
   Only Those who are Holy Can Approach
   God's Label of Choice for the New Testament Believers
   Two Ways We are Made Holy in the New Testament
   Our Double Dose of Holiness Foreshadowed
   Anointed to Serve

Chapter 9: The Intimacy of Our Approach   154
   The Three Uses of *Katenopion* in the New Testament
   Colossians 1:22—"A Marvelous Picture of Complete Purity"
   Jude 24—Our Presentation in Glory

Chapter 10: The Final Approach   169
   Laying Hold on the Hope
   The Sinai Approach and the Zion Approach
   The Heavenly Jerusalem: Revelation 21 and 22

Appendix A:
Boldness: Our Privilege as Citizens of Heaven   190

Appendix B: The Peace Offering   192

Subject Index   208

Scripture Index   212

Preface

My aim and my joy in presenting this book is to help you glimpse the Christ of unsearchable riches. When we understand what Christ has accomplished for us on the cross, we will grow in our love for and commitment to him. As our eyes open to Christ's finished work on our behalf, we will rise up to walk with God.

Much has been written about Christians' lack of purpose or vision for their own lives. "Discovering what God has put you on the planet to do," has become the rage in Christian circles. Perhaps this is symptomatic of our self-absorbed, narcissistic culture and times in which we live. When we discover what God put Christ on this planet to do, then we can rise up to fulfill God's will.

This book is not about us; it is about **HIM**. I have written this book to help you become immersed in Christ and his accomplishments at Calvary. As we view the crucifixion and resurrection of Christ and their aftereffects with precise clarity, our Christian walks will take on the power and purpose God intended. Lack of knowledge of what Christ accomplished induces the Christian to be preoccupied with lesser things. May this book help Christians to be absorbed more in Christ and less in themselves.

We must review two technical points before we begin. First, to gain an exact understanding of God's Word, it is often of great necessity to return to the Hebrew or Greek text of the Bible. One of my primary objectives is for the reader to behold the perfection and accuracy of God's Word. The Bible as originally written was God breathed, given by revelation. But man's translations are not. Hence, my concern is to restore that technical accuracy of the Scriptures by introducing the Old Testament Hebrew or the New Testament Greek when needed. My Scripture quotes are from the *King James Version* unless otherwise stated. In these Scriptural quotations I often insert Hebrew or Greek words enclosed in brackets. (The Greek and Hebrew words are put in italics transliterated into English letters. For consistency I used the *Young's Concordance* transliteration. For example, the Greek word for "boldness" in the *King James Version* in Greek letters is: παρρησια. However, like *Young's*, I used the transliterated form, *parrhēsia*.)

Secondly, on occasion, words in a Scripture quote are emphasized in **bold print** for teaching purposes. My use of bold type to call attention to a point should in no way be attributed to the Bible itself.

Leviticus and Hebrews are the "final frontier" for serious Bible students. To explain and clarify these two cornerstone books is my passion. It is not coincidence that in almost every chapter of this book, passages from both Leviticus and Hebrews are quoted and expounded upon. Understanding Leviticus and its interrelation to Hebrews and the rest of the New Testament has opened my eyes to the utter completeness of our redemption and salvation in Christ. My prayer for the reader is to ignite in you the same passion, commitment and understanding of our great salvation.

I trust this information will reinforce the underpinnings in the heart of a believer to commune with God deeper and more often. Instead of focusing on our own deficiencies, frailties, and our own less-than-perfect walks, may this book cause us to focus on Christ and His work on our behalf.

1

Introduction: Jesus Christ, the Way into God's Presence

On a hill outside Jerusalem, as the sky darkened, our Lord Jesus Christ hung on a tree. Exhausted and severely beaten, he endured an excruciating and humiliating death on a late April day in 28 AD. He was called Jesus of Nazareth, said to be from a town in Galilee. The idea of a prophet, much less the Messiah, emerging from the mud pits of northern Israel was inconceivable to the learned elite of Jerusalem.[1]

When Jesus of Nazareth laid down his life that day, it was not just another sad case of a martyr suffering a grisly death. His crucifixion was not an inescapable predicament in which he found himself; he could have avoided that hideous circumstance. Before his arrest, he could have easily evaded capture as he had done so often before. During his trials, he could have spoken out vigorously in his own defense. His oratory skill was well known, but he remained mostly silent. More significantly, he said he could have called for more than twelve legions of angels to save him in this awful hour (Matthew 26:53). This was entirely plausible considering the great power and the miracles he manifested.

The Lord Jesus Christ hung on the cross that dark day by his own free will. He allowed himself to suffer and die a shameful death to accomplish our redemption and salvation. He laid down his life by his own volition. He said to his heavenly Father, "not my will, but thine, be done." (Luke 22:42). He hung on that tree in obedience to God to fulfill all that the Old Testament Scripture had said about the coming Messiah.

> John 19:16-30:
> Then delivered he him therefore unto them to be crucified. And they took Jesus, and led *him* away.
> And he bearing his cross went forth into a place called *the place* of a skull, which is called in the Hebrew Golgotha:
> Where they crucified him, and two other with him, on either side one, and Jesus in the midst.
> And Pilate wrote a title, and put *it* on the cross. And the writing was, JESUS OF NAZARETH THE KING OF THE JEWS.
> This title then read many of the Jews: for the place where Jesus was crucified was nigh to the city: and it was written in Hebrew, *and* Greek, *and* Latin.
> Then said the chief priests of the Jews to Pilate, Write not, The King of the Jews; but that he said, I am King of the Jews.
> Pilate answered, What I have written I have written.
> Then the soldiers, when they had crucified Jesus, took his garments, and made four parts, to every soldier a part; and also *his* coat: now the coat was without seam, woven from the top throughout.
> [Verse 24] They said therefore among themselves, Let us not rend it, but cast lots for it, whose it shall be: that the scripture might be fulfilled [*plēroō*], which saith, They parted my raiment among them,

and for my vesture they did cast lots. These things therefore the soldiers did.

Now there stood by the cross of Jesus his mother, and his mother's sister, Mary the *wife* of Cleophas, and Mary Magdalene.

When Jesus therefore saw his mother, and the disciple standing by, whom he loved, he saith unto his mother, Woman, behold thy son!

Then saith he to the disciple, Behold thy mother! And from that hour that disciple took her unto his own *home*.

After this, Jesus knowing that all things were now accomplished [*teleō*], that the scripture might be fulfilled [*teleioō*], saith, I thirst.

Now there was set a vessel full of vinegar: and they filled a spunge with vinegar, and put *it* upon hyssop, and put *it* to his mouth.

When Jesus therefore had received the vinegar, he said, It is finished [*teleō*]: and he bowed his head, and gave up the ghost.

The last words our Lord uttered before his death were, "It is finished." Jesus did not say, "I am finished." When Christ said "It is finished," he was not merely referring to his life ceasing. Actually, verse 30 does not say what was finished. However, in verse 28 it clarifies what, exactly, was "finished."

> Verse 28:
> After this, Jesus knowing that all things were now accomplished [*teleō*], that the scripture might be fulfilled [*teleioō*], saith, I thirst.

What were the "all things" that "were now accomplished?" The next phrase points to the answer: ". . .that the scripture might be fulfilled [*teleioō*]. . ." The Old Testament Scriptures were finished or accomplished.

The key to understanding what this means is in these Greek words, *teleioō* and *teleō,* used in verses 28 and 30. The Greek word for "finished" is *teleō,* which could also be translated as "completed" or "accomplished." The root word of *teleō* is *telōs,* meaning "a full and complete end, not merely a cessation but fulfillment and completion."[2] What Jesus Christ "finished" or "brought to a complete and full end" in his crucifixion was the Old Testament Scripture that spoke of him. He brought to a complete and full end our redemption and salvation.[3]

The inconsistent translation in our English Bibles obscures the brilliant clarity of the Greek text. For the sake of clarity these translations of John 19:28 and 30 would be helpful:

> Verse 28: . . .Jesus knowing all things were now **completed**, that the scripture might be **completed**, saith, I thirst. . .
> Verse 30: …It is **completed!**
>
> Verse 28:. . .Jesus knowing all things were now **accomplished**, that the scripture might be **accomplished,** saith, I thirst. . .
> Verse 30: . . .It is **accomplished!**

When translated using the same word for *teleioō* and *teleō,* we readily see how verses 28 and 30 tie together.

The usual word for "fulfilled" in the New Testament is a form of the word *plēroō,* meaning to fill or make full. Please note that in John 19:24 the word for "fulfilled," in the phrase "that the scripture might be **fulfilled**," is *plēroō.* But in John 19:28 this regular word for "fulfilled," *plēroō,* is not used. Why, in verse 24, is *plēroō* used for "fulfilled" and then, just four verses later, a different word is used? Because, when our Lord said "I thirst," he knew that was the end. So, the word *teleioō* is used, which carries a sense of finality and completion. As is often the case, the technical accuracy and precision of the individual words of Scripture are astounding.

When Christ said "I thirst" in verse 28, he was not just fulfilling that one single prophecy. All the prophecies, the types, shadows and historical illustrations of the Messiah's life on earth in the Old Testament were fulfilled that day. Also, at that point he brought to full completion the Old Covenant instituted by Moses. His sacrifice terminated the Old Covenant and opened up a new age of access to God for the believer.[4]

Jesus Christ is the way into God's glorious presence. Jesus said in John 14:6, "I am the way, the truth and the life, no man cometh [approaches] unto the Father: but by me." Jesus Christ is **the** way, **the** approach to God. There is no admittance, no entrée to God, without him. Jesus Christ is **the** approach to God because he was **the** approach offering.

When Jesus Christ laid down his life on the tree at Calvary, he gave us access to God Almighty. In presenting himself as God's sacrifice for us, he became our "approach offering," opening the way into God's very presence.

> Hebrews 10:19:
> Having therefore, brethren, boldness to enter into the holiest by the blood of Jesus,

In spite of our shortcomings and sins, we have boldness to enter into the holiest by the blood of Jesus. He became the approach offering so we could enter into the holy of holies, the inner sanctum of God's magnificent presence. Under the Mosaic Law, only the high priest could enter the holy of holies of the tabernacle. This entry was performed alone and permitted only once a year. What a contrast! Now, by the sacrifice of Christ, we have boldness to enter into the holy of holies, unto the throne of grace.[5]

> Hebrews 4:16:
> Let us therefore come boldly unto the throne of grace, that we may obtain mercy, and find grace to help in time of need.

Jesus Christ opened the way into the throne room of the Father. How do we now respond to what God has done? We ought to utilize our access to God by drawing near and making our requests known. We should take our place in the presence of God. The tender heart of the Father is inviting us to commune with Him.

This free and bold access we have cost God dearly. God sacrificed the life of His only begotten Son so we could draw near to Him and have close fellowship. So let us boldly enter in and utilize what God has given by Christ.

> I John 3:1:
> Behold, what manner of love the Father hath bestowed upon us, that we should be called the sons of God: therefore the world knoweth us not, because it knew him not.

What manner of love the Father has bestowed on us—He spared not His own Son for us. We are not outcasts or rejects, but we are sons of God. We can approach our Father freely.

Access is Influence

Throughout history, access to worldly authorities has been a means of power and influence. With earthly powers, those who have had the access to that power wielded influence.

The Book of Esther provides an example of the access to worldly power and the subsequent influence.

> Esther 1:14:
> And the next unto him *was* Carshena, Shethar, Admatha, Tarshish, Meres, Marsena, *and* Memucan, the seven princes of Persia and Media, which **saw the king's face**, *and* which sat the first in the kingdom;

These seven princes "sat first in the kingdom" and constituted the highest authority in the realm. Their main power lay in their unfettered access to the monarch. They "saw the king's face." This access gave them great influence. This was in stark contrast to everyone else:

> Esther 4:11:
> All the king's servants, and the people of the king's provinces, do know, that whosoever, whether man or woman, shall come unto the king into the inner court, who is not called, *there is* one law of his to put *him* to death, except such to whom the king shall hold out the golden sceptre, that he may live: but I [Esther] have not been called to come in unto the king these thirty days.

The Persian court etiquette was meticulous and harsh. The inner court where the king sat was the throne room. Access to the Persian monarch's presence was especially difficult. To enter into the throne room uninvited and unannounced could result in death. The only people exempt from this rule were the seven princes.[6]

If you are familiar with the record of Esther, you will recall that she bravely approached unannounced and uninvited. The king accepted her entry by extending his sceptre. The life of Esther, as well as the lives of her people, hinged on this daring approach. Queen Esther could only exercise her influence **if** she had access.

These verses in Esther illustrate what is so standard throughout history. Access to the sovereign powers of this world equals the capacity to exercise power. God Almighty is the creator of heaven and earth. For us to have access to Him gives us influence and the capacity to wield power when we are in accordance with His will.

Recently in our nation's history, a political fuss arose about the issue of access to the President. In the spring of 1997 a news story broke stating that the President of the United States was holding "coffees" in the White House to give his big political contributors a chance to rub shoulders and have their picture taken with him. As the facts emerged, those who had donated $50,000 or more were invited to these gatherings with President Clinton and occasionally were permitted to stay the night in the Lincoln bedroom. These select few got to have access to, spend time with, and hopefully influence the President of the United States. This type of schmoozing is not uncommon in our form of government. What raised a fuss about the coffee klatches was that some of the attendees, who got to see and talk to the President, were sent by foreign governments. This fact was not in contention because it was not done in secret. There were pictures of these individuals with the President. So what was the big commotion about? Simply put, **Access is influence**. The grave concern was that these individuals, who represented foreign governments, might influence the President's decisions and policies. In fact, he freely admitted this is exactly what happened: "I made no policy decisions based solely on these gatherings." "Solely" is the key operative word in this quote. This is what deeply troubled people.

We have access to, and influence with, one much greater than the President. Our access to God Almighty came at extraordinary cost. The life of the Lord Jesus Christ was given in sacrifice on our behalf. The life of God's only begotten Son is worth infinitely more than $50,000! What a price has been paid on our behalf so we could have access to and influence with God!

In fact, God even <u>asks</u> us to set our petitions before Him! In real terms, this access to God gives us power and leverage. So, let's go into God's presence boldly in prayer. We have influence in the corridors of power. Why make minimal use of so valuable a resource? Jesus laid down his life for us so we could approach God boldly, not shuffling in as rejects on our own merits. We are escorted into God's presence with assurance and confidence by Jesus Christ. We have entrée into the throne room of God's grace. We have influence with God.

Why Study Old Testament Sacrifices?

A greater understanding of Old Testament offerings can enable us to grasp Jesus Christ and his perfect work of redemption more clearly. Far from an exercise in Biblical trivia, this material is thrilling because it expands our understanding of the great and wonderful salvation we have in our Lord Jesus Christ.

> Hebrews 10:1-3:
> For the law having a **shadow** of good things to come [Christ and his accomplishments], *and* not the very image of the things, can never with **those sacrifices** which they offered year by year continually make the comers thereunto perfect.
> For then would they not have ceased to be offered? because that the worshippers once purged should have had no more conscience of sins.
> But in those *sacrifices there is* a remembrance again made of sins every year.

These offerings under the law were a shadow, a silhouette, an outline of the coming Messiah who would offer himself. While these offerings were not 3-D Technicolor visuals of "good things to come," they give a shadow outline of the "once for all" sacrifice of Jesus Christ. These sacrifices were set up by God in anticipation of the true and perfect sacrifice of Jesus Christ.

God set up the offerings in the Old Testament for four basic reasons. First, they reminded people of the need for a redeemer. In offering a sacrifice, the separation, alienation and enmity from God and the sin of the offerer was brought to mind. As Hebrews 10:3 says of sacrifices, there was "a remembrance again made of sins."

Second, these offerings granted some limited cleansing or forgiveness of sins. The Old Testament trespass and sin offerings were set up for this purpose. While this subject is not the primary point of this book, it is one of the great realities of our redemption and salvation. The coming Messiah is called a trespass offering in Isaiah 53:10. In the

King James Version, "offering for sin" is the Hebrew word *asham*, and should be rendered "trespass offering."[7]

Third, <u>these offerings gave limited temporary access to God</u> and acceptance by God for the Old Testament believers. This is the point we will be looking at in this book.

In the Garden of Eden, Adam and Eve had free and unrestrained approach to God. There was no sin, sickness or death. But the relationship between God and man was shattered by the cataclysmic event in Genesis three—Adam and Eve sinned by disobeying God. The relationship they previously had with God was severed. From this point on, there was no approach to God without a sacrifice. The burnt, meal, and peace offerings were central to this purpose of approaching God.

Finally, with the offerings, <u>God pointed out to Israel the direction from which true salvation would come</u>. The sacrifice depicted an innocent victim enduring in their stead the righteous penalty for sin. As Hebrews 10:1 states, these offerings were a shadow outline of the coming Messiah who would offer himself. The Old Testament sacrifices foreshadowed, represented, or portrayed Jesus Christ and his accomplishments as our complete sacrifice. Like an architect's blueprints, they defined and gave shape to the coming Redeemer and his work. Just as an architect sketches the plans on paper, the Old Testament offerings gave a detailed drawing or conception of the Christ who was to come.

These four points were God's original intent. However, we should take a moment to consider how God's original purposes for the offerings were subverted by the unbelief and ignorance of the offerers. Sadly, in time, the Israelites forgot much of God's original intent and purpose for the sacrifices. The offerings were degraded into self-righteous works without heart, reverence, or believing toward God. Paradoxically, the great lesson of sacrifices was that it was not by works. Although the preparation and presentation of offerings for sacrifice involved work, the basic point was that the approach to God was not by one's own good deeds. The vital point of a sacrifice was the transference of the offerer's sin onto the offering. The innocent blood of the sacrifice was shed in the stead of the offerer. All the wrath and the enmity that stood between the offerer and God was heaped upon the sacrifice. Then it died as a substitute. Ironically, the message implicit in every sacrifice was that no dead works would avail to bring one into God's presence.

However, by the time Psalms were written, David said by revelation:

> Psalm 40:6:
> Sacrifice and offering thou didst not desire; mine ears hast thou opened: burnt offering and sin offering hast thou not required.

Here in Psalms, God says He did not desire or require offerings. To keep this statement in perspective, the writer of this psalm is the same individual who helped re-institute the temple worship, priesthood, and the sacrifices, which were later carried out in Solomon's Temple (I Chronicles 23-26).

At one point, God did desire offerings or He would not have set them up in the first place. If done with a pure heart and right believing, they pleased Him. In Leviticus chapter one, the burnt offering was to be a "sweet savour unto the Lord." "Sweet savour" means a soothing or pleasing fragrance. So these offerings had the capacity to please God. But, sadly, the right believing and understanding was lost, so God no longer desired the offerings.

In our time of the New Testament, we face similar situations concerning the misuse and misunderstanding of things God has set up in His Word. For example, I Corinthians 11 reproves the church for losing the right believing concerning holy communion and the consequences of that loss.[8] Another principle God set up, which is often misunderstood or the full greatness of is not believed, is abundant sharing or financial giving. Interestingly, financial sharing is closely paralleled to Old Testament sacrifices:

> Philippians 4:18:
> But I have all, and abound: I am full, having received of Epaphroditus the things *which were sent* from you, an odour of a sweet smell, a sacrifice acceptable, wellpleasing to God.

Abundant sharing, as well as Communion, when done with a heart of dedication and accurate Scriptural believing, brings tremendous profit. Yet how sad it is, due to wrong teaching or ignorance, that so many Christians have not tapped into the immense benefits. In a similar way, the significance and benefits of sacrifices in the Old Testament was lost.

In this book, we will consider the approach offerings of the Old Testament and how they foreshadowed Christ. This was indeed the great purpose of the Old Testament offerings and sacrifices; they continually served to point the Old Covenant believers to the coming Savior. We will see that these offerings depicted the characteristics and the accomplishments of the coming Messiah.

Jesus Christ as our "approach offering" is dramatically prefigured in the Old Testament sacrifices. In the next chapter, we will consider how the offerings in Leviticus portray Jesus Christ as our approach offering. While the Mosaic sacrifices are only faint copies or shadows of he who was to come, they do shed light on God's desire and plan of the ages: to have the way open into His presence so His people can have full fellowship with Him.

Have you ever heard the old expression, "His reach exceeded his grasp?" It refers to someone being able to reach or attain to something but then not having the strength to grasp or grab or take possession. Someone may make a valiant effort but then not have what it takes to succeed.

This is so often true of us as Christians. Often we reach out for something, but we are not able to grasp it. We may understand enough to attempt something for God—but lack the internal strength to grab it or stick to it. For example, we may resolve to spend more time and effort in prayer. We may plan to make a daily effort to spend time in quiet fellowship with our heavenly Father. But somehow, in the long run, it never materializes. The best of intentions do not give us the strength of character and capacity of mind to succeed.

My purpose with this book is to strengthen your grasp of the Word of God—to add some weight and force to your perception of our approach to God. I want to build this subject for you, so you can tip the scales in your believing from mental assent to full certainty. I am sure, as you grow in your knowledge, the strength of your conviction and capacity to believe will grow. As you dwell in this subject in the Scriptures, in the deepest part of your heart you will say: "I can approach God."

Notes

1. John 7:41, 52. The first negative comment about Galilee recorded in Scripture is in I Kings 9:11-13. King Hiram voiced his displeasure at the region after receiving some Galilean cities as a gift from King Solomon. He called the area, "Cabul" which in Hebrew sounds like "good for nothing." (NIV note on I Kings 9:13). In John 1:46 Nathanael's initial response concerning Jesus was, "Can there any good thing come out of Nazareth." Edersheim stated: ". . .The unmitigated contempt with which they [of Jerusalem] were wont to speak of Galilee, and of the Galileans. . .of the utter abhorrence with which they regarded the unlettered country-people." Edersheim, *The Life and Times of Jesus the Messiah*, Volume I (New York: Longmans, 1901), 114. Our Savior understood rejection and what it was like to start out at the bottom rung of the ladder.

2. E. W. Bullinger, *Critical Lexicon* (London: Bagster, 1974), 248.

3. The profound accuracy and precision of the Greek tense here is stunning. The Greek word, *teleō*, in verses 28 and 30 is in the perfect indicative tense. In Greek "the perfect tense is the tense of completed action." It is understood as, "the point of culmination and the existence of its finished results." "It implies a process, but views that process as having reached its consummation and existing in a present result." In John 19:30 Christ's offering was completed. The phrase "It is written" is also in this perfect tense. (H. E. Dana and Julius Mantey, *A Manual Grammar of the Greek New Testament* (New York: The MacMillan Company, 1955), 200.

4. In chapter five, we examine how the rent veil signified the complete end of the Old Covenant.

5. Our access to the throne and our entrance to God's dwelling place is of such vital importance because this is where our help comes from. Repeatedly, in the Old Testament, help and deliverance came from God's dwelling place. With access to God comes deliverance. These references cite examples of the delivering power in approaching God in His dwelling place: Psalm 20:2, 6; Psalm 18:6-16; Psalm 102:1, 2, 18, 19; I Kings 8:38 and 39; II Chronicles 20:8 and 9; Jonah 2:4-7. God could hear the cry of His Old Testament believers from His holy place. But their entry was restricted. We can boldly enter in.

6. James M. Freeman, *Manners and Customs of the Bible* (Plainfield: NJ: Logos International, 1972), 205. Lamsa says this strict rule of access to the king protected him from assassination. George M. Lamsa, *Old Testament Light* (Philadelphia, Holman, 1978, 1st edition, 1964), 408.

7. David Bergey, *Our Identification with Christ's Sacrifice* (Redlands: CA, 2000) 42-43.

8. David Bergey, *Our Identification with Christ's Sacrifice*, 20-37. This topic of holy communion and how it relates to Old Testament sacrifices is explained extensively in this publication.

2

Leviticus: Approaching God with an Approach Offering

Although Leviticus is one of the most obscure and unread books of the Bible, it reflects the heart of a loving God who desires that His people approach Him and have fellowship with Him. The same God that authored the New Testament authored Leviticus. The same heart of God that pulses through the New Testament beats in Leviticus. His desire was and is to commune, to fellowship, with His people. Sacrifices and offerings were set up so the believers under the Old Covenant could have some measure of approach and access to God.

Although much of the Book of Leviticus deals with the various sacrifices, the first seven chapters were especially significant for the individual Old Testament believer. In Leviticus 1-7, God made available five different sacrifices for the individual believer to perform. These sacrifices were not national or public offerings solely carried out by the priests. These were individual sacrifices brought to the priest, before the Lord, by the initiative of the individual believer.

The Two Functions of the Five Offerings of Leviticus 1-7

The five different sacrifices of Leviticus 1-7:
1. Burnt offering.
2. Meat offering. In a bizarre twist of archaic English word usage, the only offering in Leviticus 1-7 with **no meat** is the "meat offering." Since, in our current usage, "meat" means the flesh of an animal, this offering will be rendered "meal offering."
3. Peace offering.
4. Sin offering. The traditional rabbinical name was the purification offering or purgation offering.[1]
5. Trespass offering.

These five sacrifices, while distinct in themselves, performed two basic functions and can be divided into two general categories. The burnt, meal, and peace offerings were offered for a "sweet savour" unto the Lord. In the Hebrew language the word for "savour" means fragrance or odor. The word for "sweet" means soothing, satisfaction or delight. Therefore, "sweet savour unto the Lord" can more accurately be translated as "satisfying odor to the Lord"[2] or "aroma pleasing to the Lord."[3] Thus the term "sweet savour" indicated approaching God to give Him a sense of satisfaction and delight.[4] With these offerings, the Old Testament believer approached God to bring a soothing fragrance to Him—to bless God with a pleasing aroma. The term "sweet savour" is mentioned many times in the context of these three offerings.[5]

In contrast, the sin and trespass offerings were to obtain forgiveness for, and purification from, sins. The trespass offering involved payment and restitution for sins committed. With the burnt, meal, and peace offering the Old Covenant believer approached God to fellowship with

Him. With the sin and trespass offerings, they came to God as sinful and impure. The purpose of these offerings was to re-establish fellowship with God and for purification, cleansing and forgiveness.[6]

Two Categories of Offerings

Offerings	Category	Purpose
Burnt, Meal, Peace	**Sweet Savor:**	To bless and please God; to approach God in fellowship and prayer
Sin, Trespass	**Sin:**	To obtain forgiveness and purification; to re-establish fellowship with God

What a wonderful God! He had such love and concern for His people that He engineered a detailed system of sacrifices so His chosen covenant people could approach Him and obtain cleansing and forgiveness. Here in Leviticus, God lovingly instituted these sacrifices so He could connect with His people and bring them into fellowship with Him.

These wonderful offerings stood as an open invitation for the Old Testament believer to approach God. While these sacrifices were of some assistance in enabling people to approach God and obtain some cleansing and covering of sin, they were only a faint outline of he who was to come: the Lord Jesus Christ.

In these sacrifices, instituted by revelation, God portrayed and foreshadowed the coming Christ. This is what made these sacrifices in the Old Testament such an integral and vital part of the Word of God. With these offerings, God pointed toward the manner in which true salvation would come. Namely, a sinless victim would endure, in their stead, the penalty for sin. These multiple animal sacrifices repeatedly portrayed the one-time act of the coming Christ who would, in due time, sacrifice himself for mankind.

Jesus Christ, as the consummate offering for all time, completely fulfilled both aspects of these offerings. The New Testament revelation declares him to be both sweet savour offering **and** sin offering.

> Ephesians 5:2
> And walk in love, as Christ also hath loved us, and hath given himself for us an offering and a sacrifice to God for a **sweetsmelling savour**.

Jesus Christ was a sweet savour offering to God.

> Hebrews 9:28:
> So Christ was once offered to **bear the sins** of many…

He also bore sins as a sin offering. The two general functions of these Levitical offerings reflect the two primary accomplishments of our redemption by Christ.

What these Levitical offerings accomplished for the Old Covenant believer, in part and in shadow, the offering of Christ accomplished for the New Covenant believer in fullness and perfection. We have full approach to God **and** total cleansing from sin. These are two of the paramount realities of the New Covenant. While the cleansing and purification from sin by Christ's sacrifice is one of the greatest truths of life, our main emphasis in this book is on our approach to God.

Approaching God with an Approach Offering

The focus of this study is on how these offerings of Leviticus anticipate Christ in his role as our approach offering.

> Leviticus 1:1 and 2:
> And the LORD called unto Moses, and spake unto him out of the tabernacle of the congregation, saying,
> Speak unto the children of Israel, and say unto them...

God called unto Moses. God spoke to him. God took the initiative. These sacrifices of Leviticus 1-7 were God's idea. God initiated and then arranged this system of sacrifices. Moses did not institute these sacrifices on his own as part of a political effort to gain control over a tribal confederation. He set up these sacrifices because God called and spoke to him directly "out of the tabernacle." God told Moses how to institute these sacrifices in precise detail.

Moses was not the first to establish a sacrificial system in the ancient world. By the time of Moses, many city-states of the ancient world had sacrificial systems, priesthoods, and temples. Moses was not original in this respect. However, he was original, in that he wrote down—by direct revelation from God—how to conduct the sacrifices, point by point. God guided Moses down to the last exact detail. This sacrificial system that provided for an approach to God looked forward to The Approach, The Way, the Lord Jesus Christ.

Leviticus 1:2:
Speak unto the children of Israel, and say unto them, If any man of you bring [*qarab*] an offering [*qorban*] unto the Lord, ye shall bring [*qarab*] your offering [*qorban*] of the cattle, *even* of the herd, and of the flock.

Both of the phrases "bring an offering" and "ye shall bring your offering" are made up of two related Hebrew words: *qarab* and *qorban*. <u>*Qarab* is the verb</u> meaning to bring near or to approach. <u>*Qorban* is the noun</u> literally meaning a bringing near, or an approach. The verb *qarab*, is the root word of *qorban*. This root word, *qarab*, demonstrates the underlying meaning and function of *qorban*: an approach offering to God. So, the literal sense of the word *qorban* is an approach offering. A literal translation of "bring your offering" would be "approach with your approach offering." Our English versions do not capture the essence of what is so graphic in the Hebrew text. The Strong's numbering system conveys how closely these two words are related. The number of *qarab* is 7126, and the number of *qorban* is 7133.[7]

Qarab: **to approach, bring near or draw near,**
<u>verb</u> (Strong's # 7126)

***Qorban*:** **an approach (offering),**
<u>noun</u> (Strong's # 7133)

Since *qorban* is derived from the root verb *qarab,* the underlying and root idea of a *qorban* is related to approaching and drawing near. The original intent of *qorban* is an offering with the specific function of approaching God. The noun, *qorban,* literally means "an approach."

In E. W. Bullinger's *The Companion Bible*, the note on Leviticus 1:2 renders "offering," *qorban,* as "admittance, entrance, or access offering." Appendix 43 of *The Companion Bible* further defines *qorban* as, "*a gift,* or *an admittance-offering*: It is the present brought . . . in order to secure an audience, or to see the face of the superior, and find access into his presence. Hence. . .the face-offering…essentially an admittance-offering; securing the entrée."

While the literal meaning of *qorban* is approach offering, in the Bible this same word is broadly used for gifts, offerings, and sacrifices. *Young's Concordance* translates *qorban* as "what is brought near." *Qorban* is a general term for anything brought near. Yet, the underlying idea of this word *qorban*—as derived from its root word *qarab*—suggests an approach, a drawing near to God. [8]

The basic underlying function of these offerings in Leviticus was to offer some limited access to God. God's original intent with the *qorban* offerings was to enable His people to come before Him. The Old Covenant believers had no open access into the holy of holiest—into the very presence of God. However, they could come before God, before His tabernacle, and later His temple, to offer sacrifice to Him.

Psalm 65:4:
Blessed *is the man whom* thou choosest, and causest to approach [*qarab*] *unto thee, that* he may dwell in thy courts: we shall be satisfied with the goodness of thy house, *even* of thy holy temple.

This verse in Psalms speaks of approaching God and dwelling in the courts of the temple. The courts of the temple were the enclosed temple area, not the holy place or the holy of holies. As wonderful as the Old Testament believers were, the best they could do was enter in the courts of the Lord. The closest they could approach was the courts! The court of the tabernacle, or later the temple, is where the people of God brought their sacrifices to be offered.

Psalm 100:4:
Enter into his gates with thanksgiving, *and* into his courts with praise: be thankful unto him, and bless his name.

We as sons and daughters of God don't just enter into His gates or into His courts, we walk straight into the holy of holies, into the very presence of God! It was unavailable for most Old Testament believers to approach beyond the gates and the courts. Access to the inner rooms of the tabernacle was restricted. Yet Hebrews 11 says Old Testament believers "through faith subdued kingdoms, wrought righteousness, obtained promises, stopped the mouths of lions. . ." This was the Old Covenant believer at his best. Yet, these notable men and women could not approach beyond the courts. They could not enter into the holy of holies, into the very presence of God.[9] Yet what miracles God worked for them. All of their remarkable works of believing could not bring access into the holy of holies. It is only by the believing work of the Lord Jesus

Christ that we now have bold fearless access into the very throne room of the Father. While the Old Testament believers did mighty works, it is only by the finished work of Jesus Christ that our full and continuous access to God is accomplished.

The word, *qorban*, and its associated verb form, *qarab*, both enunciate the general function of these Levitical offerings—to approach God with an approach offering. But these words also point toward a greater and future reality. These approach offerings in Leviticus serve as shadows, as faint outlines of the coming Savior. Just as an architect sketches out his plans, so God, the architect of our redemption, constructed a detailed illustration of the coming redeemer. These offerings did not complete man's relationship to God. However, they point directly to he who did—Christ.

Next, we will see how these words *qarab* and *qorban* used together form a figure of speech, which indicate a point of strong emphasis in God's Word.

To Approach, *Qarab*, Emphasized by the Figure of Speech, *Polyptoton*

> Leviticus 1:2:
> Speak unto the children of Israel, and say unto them, If any man of you bring [*qarab*] an offering [*qorban*] unto the Lord, ye shall bring [*qarab*] your offering [*qorban*] of the cattle, *even* of the herd, and of the flock.

These two related words, *qarab* and *qorban,* used together in a phrase form a figure of speech by repetition called *Polyptoton*. In the repetition of these related words, the emphasis falls on the verb *qarab*, **to approach**. The usage of this figure of speech heralds and amplifies the overarching subject of the opening seven chapters of Leviticus—approaching God. Whether Leviticus or Hebrews, Old Covenant or New, God's big concern is for His people to approach Him.

Sadly, the study of figures of speech in the Bible has not received the attention it deserves in Christian circles. In spite of E.W. Bullinger's monumental work on this subject of over a thousand pages, *Figures of Speech Used in the Bible*, most Biblical scholars ignore this field. The average Christian regards a Biblical figure of speech as weakening the meaning where it is used. The term "figures of speech" is often synonymous for "dust bin" where difficult to understand verses are put. Nothing could be farther from the truth.

On the contrary, figures of speech in the Bible draw attention to and intensify the sense of a passage. Understanding this is exciting because we can now see where God places His emphasis in His Word. Today, we may use exclamation points, bold print, or yellow highlighters to add emphasis. Our modern use of figures of speech is haphazard and limited. The ancient languages, however, had a vast and intricate system of figures of speech to give weight and add intensity to a word or expression. Actually, these figures of speech in the Bible are the Holy Spirit's markings on points of emphasis in the Scriptures.

One common way a figure of speech is formed is by repetition. Figures of speech involving some form of repetition abound in the Scriptures. E.W. Bullinger, in his book on figures of speech, spends over two hundred pages examining various figures involving repetition. He cataloged almost fifty different figures that involve repetition of some kind.

When God says in Leviticus, "If any man of you approach with an approach offering," He is using a figure of speech involving repetition to mark out an important point. The repetition of these related words, *qorban* and *qarab*, is deliberately used by God to draw attention to these words and what they communicate. The reader is to take notice and pay attention.

The pairing of *qarab* with its associated noun, *qorban*, is not a mere coincidence or a common idiomatic Hebrew expression here in Leviticus 1:2. These repetitions of *qorban* and *qarab* are not accidental. They are not just a stylistic flourish of the Hebrew language. This pairing of *qarab* with its associated noun, *qorban*, forms a figure of speech giving emphasis and intensity. It was done intentionally to call attention to one overarching theme—approach.

Qarab and *qorban* occur together in the same phrase nineteen times in the first seven chapters of Leviticus forming a figure of speech. This calls attention to the central idea of Leviticus 1-7—"Approach with an approach offering."

However, the deliberate clarity of the originally-given Word of God in Leviticus is obscured by translation. The exact root meaning of these words, *qorban* and *qarab*, and the figure of speech they form when used together, are almost completely hidden in the English versions.

The figure of speech formed by *qarab* coupled with *qorban* in the same phrase, is called *Polyptoton*. *Polyptoton* can be translated into the English as "Many Inflections."

Polyptoton brings attention to itself <u>by repetition</u>. It occurs when words which have the same root are repeated in different forms. In Leviticus this figure is used with *qarab* and *qorban* to emphasize the Old Covenant believer approaching God with these approach offerings.

Polyptoton: "Many Inflections"
The repetition of the same word
 in different forms.

Polyptoton adds emphasis and intensity.

An example of *Polyptoton* is in Genesis 2:17, "But of the tree of the knowledge of good and evil, thou shalt not eat of it: for in the day that thou eatest thereof thou shalt surely die." "Thou shalt surely die," more literally from the Hebrew is, "**dying thou shalt die**." The repetition of the verb in the forms "die" and "dying," forms the figure *Polyptoton*. The emphasis then falls on the verb, "die."[10]

As one can see, the problem with this figure of speech is that it is usually obscured, being lost in the English versions. Translations attempt to capture the sense of the meaning of a passage, not to give a literal translation. In Genesis 2:17 the translators added intensity to the verb by adding the adverb, "surely." They deserve credit for perceiving the emphasis of this figure of repetition contained in "dying thou shalt die." They rendered it, "Thou shalt surely die."[11]

In Leviticus, "approach with an approach offering" places the emphasis on the verb.[11] When *qorban* and *qarab* are paired together, the noun, *qorban,* serves to accentuate the verb, *qarab*. When Leviticus 1:2 says "approach with your approach offering" the verb "approach" is then to be understood in the superlative sense. The action of approaching is where the most careful attention is to be given. The most emphatic focus should be placed on the approach. The act of approaching the Lord God is marked out with this figure declaring the "magnitude and gravity" of this approach to God and the "greatness and importance of its results."[12]

While this figure amplifies the dominant subject of the first seven chapters of Leviticus, the subject of approaching God continues throughout the book. The banner title over much of this Book of Leviticus could be, "Approaching God." This figure is in no way a red herring set at cross purposes with the overall context of Leviticus. This figure fits harmoniously with the immediate and the remote context in which it is set. Chapter 10 relates the illegitimate approach of Aaron's sons. In chapter 16 the Day of Atonement is instituted with the approach of the high priest once a year. The feasts of Leviticus deal with the nation of Israel approaching three times each year.

Profoundly, in a larger sense, **the approach** unto God is the great banner issue of the ages. The opening of Genesis establishes the free approach of Adam and Eve to God and the loss of that access. The closing of Revelation explains how all things are made new and the approach to God is reestablished. God's yearning desire, from cover to cover of the Scripture, is for His people to approach and fellowship with Him.

This figure, *Polyptoton*, although obscured by translation, gives force and intensity to this momentous issue. Since the creation of Adam, God's utmost will and desire has been to be with His people. This figure, while buried in the

Hebrew text, resonates from Leviticus 1:2 all the way to Hebrews 10:19. Today under the New Covenant, we **still** approach God by an approach offering—Jesus Christ.

In the next chapter we will examine the two dominant Hebrew verbs of Leviticus 1-7—*qarab* and *qatar*. Understanding what they mean and how they are used will enable us to continue to unlock the great truths of the opening chapters of Leviticus.

Notes

1. *Tanakh The Holy Scriptures, the New JPS Translation According to the Traditional Hebrew Text* (The Jewish Publication Society, 1985), 156. Also see Jacob Milgrom, *The Anchor Bible, Leviticus 1-16*, (Doubleday, 1991), 226-318.

2. *The Amplified Bible.*

3. *New International Version.*

4. The term "sweet savour," meaning soothing fragrance or pleasing aroma, is the figure of speech *condescensio*, where human characteristics are given to God. Here the sense of smell is attributed to the Almighty. These offerings were to bring a sense of satisfaction or delight to God just as certain smells do to humans. E. W. Bullinger, *Figures of Speech Used in the Bible* (Grand Rapids: MI: Baker, reprint ed. 1968), 871.

5. Burnt offering: Lev. 1:,13,17. Meal offering: Lev. 2:2,9. Peace offering: Lev. 3:5, 16.

6. Andrew Jukes, *The Law of the Offerings* (Grand Rapids: MI: Kregel, 1st American edition, 1966).

7. In the Analytical Hebrew Lexicon, *qorban* is listed under the root word, *qarab*, indicating that the noun *qorban* is derived from *qarab*. Qarab is the root word of *qorban*. Benjamin Davidson, *The Analytical Hebrew and Chaldee Lexicon*, (Grand Rapids: MI: Zondervan, reprint ed. 1970), 666.

8. Charles H. Welch, *In Heavenly Places* (London: Berean Publishing Trust), 248. Every usage of *qorban* cannot be termed "approach offering." Its usages are too broad. However, the *qorban* of Leviticus 1-3 are approach offerings and can be referred to as such. Not only because of etymology but because of context and usage in these chapters. In Mark 7:11 there is mention of "corban" that is a reference to the Hebrew word, *qorban*. Here in Mark, *qorban* is used in its broader usage as a gift.

9. There were some notable exceptions to this restricted access in the Old Testament. As we shall examine in chapter five, the prominent exception was high priest entering in once a year on the Day of Atonement,. But perhaps the most phenomenal exception is the event of Exodus 24:8-11. Immediately after Moses ratified the covenant by sprinkling the blood, Moses, and Aaron, Nadab, and Abihu, and seventy of the elders of Israel ascended up Mt. Sinai. Exodus 24:10 and 11 says what happened next: "And they saw the God of Israel: and there was under his feet as it were a paved work of a sapphire stone, and as it were the body of heaven in his clearness. . . also they saw God, and did eat and drink."

After being sprinkled with the blood of the covenant, they were totally purified and holy. Only then could they ascend with Moses into the very presence of God. They were a purified people who had not yet broken the covenant.

Here is a glimpse at a scene unequaled under the Old Covenant. There is no parallel to this event until the coming of Christ. Individual priests and prophets saw God's glory in the Old Testament. But here it was not a privileged individual, but the seventy elders of Israel, representing the whole nation. They not only beheld God, but they also "did eat and drink." They were altogether at ease, on most intimate terms. They enjoyed for a brief moment what is ours forever! This glorious moment in Exodus 24 was a foretaste of what is ours in Christ continuously. This record is a glimpse at God's will for all His people.

However, the initial glory of the Old Covenant was soon overcome by sin and treachery. Just weeks later the Children of Israel made a golden calf to worship (Exodus 32). Such is the frailty of man.

10. Chris Geer, *Walking in God's Power® foundational class Students Study Guide* (Stirling: Scotland, Word Promotions Ltd. 1995), 139.

11. *The Companion Bible* in its note on Genesis 20:28 gives a number of examples of the *King James Version* translator's correct handling of the figure *Polyptoton*. However, as we have seen, this figure was completely overlooked by the translators where *qarab* was coupled with *qorban* in Leviticus 1-7.

12. As with many figures of speech, *Polyptoton,* has various forms. "Approach with an approach offering" in Leviticus as well as "dying thou shalt die" in Genesis 2:17 is the variety of *Polyptoton* where the verb is used with a related noun. E. W. Bullinger, *Figures of Speech Used in the Bible*, page 275 describes this form of *Polyptoton*:

> **Verbs with cognate [related] noun:**
> A verb and a cognate [related] noun are used together, when great emphasis is placed upon the assertion or expression. It is a kind of **superlative degree in verbs** to declare the magnitude and gravity of an action or the greatness and importance of its results.

The emphasis is placed on the verb.

3

Approaching God in Prayer

In this chapter we will see that the underlying but central message of the opening chapters of Leviticus is approaching God in prayer. To uncover this truth we will examine the usage and definition of the two dominant Hebrew verbs in this section—*qarab* and *qatar*. First, we will look at *qarab,* to approach, used 19 times with the figure, *Polyptoton*. Then, we will examine the Hebrew verb, *qatar,* meaning to burn as incense. This verb, *qatar,* is used over 20 times in the context of the burnt, meal, and peace offerings.

While working through Hebrew word studies seems laborious at first, seeing the simplicity of Leviticus will be the end result. Doing "word studies" in the Bible often has a major pitfall. They put the weight on a single word by itself, rather than the context. However, the constant repetition of the two verbs, *qarab* and *qatar,* in this narrow context points us to the overarching message of these opening chapters of Leviticus. This is not meaningless redundancy; rather God is obviously trying to teach us something!

The study of these Hebrew words is not meant to weary the reader, but to carefully document and reveal the true message of Leviticus—to approach God in prayer. But we should never forget the most profound, broadest contextual point of these sacrifices—Christ. As Hebrews 10:1 says, these sacrifices were a shadow of that which was to come.

Qarab, To Approach

As previously stated, in the first seven chapters of Leviticus the approach unto God is emphasized by the figure of speech *Polyptoton*. Nineteen times this figure of speech is formed by *qarab* and *qorban* being used together in the same phrase.[1] God continually drives home the primary object of the offerings—to approach Him. God's deep concern was to institute a system whereby some measure of approach and fellowship could be had by the individual believer until Jesus Christ, the true approach to God, could be made manifest.

Again, let us look at the opening lines of Leviticus.

> Leviticus 1:2:
> Speak unto the children of Israel, and say unto them, If any man of you bring an offering [**approach with an approach offering**] unto the Lord, ye shall bring your offering [**approach with your approach offering**] of the cattle, even of the herd, and of the flock.

Although indiscernible in the English versions, this figure, *Polyptoton*, emphasizes the approach unto God. Here, this phrase—approach with an approach offering—is repeated twice and establishes this dominant theme: approach. Even if it had only occurred once, it should have arrested our attention. Whether in the Old Covenant or New, "approaching God by an approach offering" is one of the preeminent subjects of the Word of God.

The burnt offering in chapter one of Leviticus has four occurrences of *qarab* coupled with *qorban*:

> 1:3: If his offering [*qorban*] *be* a burnt sacrifice of the herd, let him offer [*qarab*] a male without blemish: he shall offer [*qarab*] it. . .
> 1:10: And if his offering [*qorban*] *be* of the flocks, *namely*, of the sheep, or of the goats, for a burnt sacrifice; he shall bring [*qarab*] it a male without blemish.[2]
> 1:14: And if the burnt sacrifice for his offering [*qorban*] to the LORD *be* of fowls, then he shall bring [*qarab*] his offering [*qorban*] of turtledoves, or of young pigeons.
> 1:15: And the priest shall bring [*qarab*] it unto the altar, and wring off his head, and burn *it* on the altar; and the blood thereof shall be wrung out at the side of the altar:

In the Hebrew text, the last word of verse 14 is *qorban,* and the first word of verse 15 is *qarab*; thus forming the figure a second time in these two verses. A literal translation to indicate the position of the words would read, ". . . turtledoves, or of young pigeons, his **approach offering**. **Approach** to the altar the priest. . ." The noun and the verb are next to each other in the Hebrew text, although this is not evident from the sentence structure in the English Bibles.

The meal offering in chapter two, like the burnt offering, has four uses of this figure: [3]

> 2:1: And when any will offer [*qarab*] a meat offering unto the Lord, his offering [*qorban*] shall be *of* fine flour; and he shall pour oil upon it, and put frankincense thereon.
> 2:4: And if thou bring [*qarab*] an oblation [*qorban*] of a meat offering. . .

> 2:12: As for the oblation [*qorban*] of the firstfruits, ye shall offer [*qarab*] them unto the LORD: but they shall not be burnt on the altar for a sweet savour.
> 2:13: . . .with all thine offerings [*qorban*] thou shalt offer [*qarab*] salt.

In Leviticus chapter three, the peace offering opens up with this preeminent figure of speech. *Polyptoton* headlines chapters one, two, and three with the same idea of approaching God with an approach offering. This figure magnifies the overall purpose of the burnt, meal, and peace offerings. In the first verse of each of these three chapters, this figure of speech heralds the central subject of each chapter—approach to God.

> 3:1: And if his oblation [*qorban*] *be* a sacrifice of peace offering, if he offer [*qarab*] *it* of the herd; whether *it be* a male or female, he shall offer [*qarab*] it without blemish before the Lord.
> 3:6: And if his offering [*qorban*] for a sacrifice of peace offering unto the LORD *be* of the flock; male or female, he shall offer *[qarab]* it without blemish.
> 3:7: If he offer [*qarab*, approach] an lamb for his offering [*qorban*], then shall he offer [qarab, *approach*] it before the Lord.

In verse seven in the Hebrew text, a remarkable **triple** use of *qarab* and *qorban* occurs in immediate succession! This rough working translation shows the order of the words in the Hebrew text: "If with a lamb he **approaches** with his **approach offering, approach** he shall, before the Lord."

This is a rare triple "conjunction" which amplifies a subject of great magnitude in God's Word. In astronomy, a planetary conjunction occurs when heavenly bodies line up along an imaginary straight line with the North Star.[4] The

North Star is called the guiding star since it orients the night traveler in the correct direction. When a triple planetary conjunction occurs in the heavens, it is widely reported by the news media. Planetariums offer visitors a view of the event through their powerful telescopes. Enthusiasts travel away from the city lights with their telescopes for a clearer view. Just as the heavens, God's Word is one of the works of God. More exciting than a triple planetary conjunction are these three words of Leviticus 3:7. These three words, like a triple planetary conjunction, are in straight alignment with the paramount guiding subject of all Scripture—the Lord Jesus Christ. The minute detail of the Word of God is thrilling.

> 3:12: And if his offering [*qorban*] be a goat, then he shall offer [*qarab*] it...
> 3:14: And he shall offer [*qarab*] thereof his offering [*qorban*]..."
> 7:13: Besides the cakes, he shall offer [*qarab*] for his offering [*qorban*] leavened bread with the sacrifice of thanksgiving of his peace offerings.
> 7:14: And of it he shall offer [*qarab*] one out of the whole oblation [*qorban*] for... the peace offerings.
> 7:16: But if the sacrifice of his offering [*qorban*] be a vow, or a voluntary offering, it shall be eaten the same day that he offereth [*qarab*] his sacrifice...
> 7:29: .. He that offereth [*qarab*] the sacrifice of his peace offerings unto the LORD shall bring his oblation [*qorban*] ... of his peace offerings.

The figure of speech, *Polyptoton*, formed by *qarab* and *qorban* has been abundantly applied to the burnt, peace, and meal offerings. Yet, this figure is not used in the context of the sin or trespass offerings. Although the sin or trespass offerings are referred to as a *qorban* on occasion, the emphasis of these offerings was not the approach.

Rather, the function of the sin or trespass offerings was for forgiveness and purification.

Chapter 7 of Leviticus closes out with this section of Scripture using this figure:

> Leviticus 7:37 and 38:
> This *is* the law of the burnt offering, of the meat [meal] offering, and of the sin offering, and of the trespass offering, and of the consecrations, and of the sacrifice of the peace offerings;
> Which the Lord commanded Moses in the mount Sinai, in the day that he commanded the children of Israel to offer their oblations [**approach with an approach offering**] unto the Lord, in the wilderness of Sinai.

These two closing verses review each subject covered in the last seven chapters: the burnt offering, the meal offering, the sin offering, the trespass offering, the consecrations of the priests, and the peace offering. Both the opening two verses of Leviticus chapter one and the closing two verses of Leviticus seven contain the figure of speech, "approach with an approach offering." This powerful figure bookends this section of Scripture.

Could God's repeated emphasis on **the approach** to Him be any stronger or more emphatic? If God had marked this subject by this figure just once, it would have been worthy of our notice and thoughtful examination. Instead, so no one would ever miss the point, God pounded it home nineteen times. It is tragic that figures of speech in the Bible have been so rarely appreciated. In this study, we have re-captured a portion of understanding in the field of figures of speech. But, more importantly, this examination has enabled us to understand the foremost object of the sacrifices here in Leviticus 1-7. This has opened to us

God's heart, God's desire: that His people are given access, approach to Him. God's desire extends from one end of Scripture to the other. Whether in the Old or in the New Testament, God wants to supply an approach offering so His people can approach Him.

Qatar, To Burn as Incense

Now let us consider the word *qatar* and the central message it conveys. The verb, *qatar*, means to burn incense.[5] *Qatar* is the verb form of the common word used for incense in the Hebrew Old Testament.[6] *Qatar* means to burn incense, to offer fragrance conveying the sense of producing a pleasing aroma, a sweet fragrance unto God.[7]

The burnt offering of Leviticus chapter one is *qatar*: burned as incense unto God.

1:9: "...burn [*qatar*, burn as incense] all on the altar..."
1:13: "...burn [*qatar*, burn as incense] *it* upon the altar..."
1:15: "...burn [*qatar*, burn as incense] *it* on the altar..."
1:17: "...burn [*qatar*, burn as incense] it upon the altar..."

In chapter two, the portion of the meal offering combined with frankincense—which is "incense"—is *qatar*: burned as incense upon the altar.

2:2: "...burn [*qatar*, burn as incense] the memorial of it upon the altar..."
2:9: "...burn [*qatar*, burn as incense] *it* upon the altar..."
2:11: "...for ye shall burn [*qatar*, burn as incense] no leaven..."
2:16: "...burn [*qatar*, burn as incense] the memorial of it ..."

With the peace offerings and sin offerings, the fat is separated from the sacrifice and then *qatar*: burnt as incense upon the altar.

3:5: "...burn [*qatar*, burn as incense] it on the altar..."
3:11: "...burn [*qatar*, burn as incense] it upon the altar..."
3:16: "...burn [*qatar*, burn as incense] them upon the altar..."
4:10: "...burn [*qatar*, burn as incense] them upon the altar..."
4:19: "...burn [*qatar*, burn as incense] *it* upon the altar..."

These verses are only some of the uses of this word *qatar* in the context of offerings. While the main point of the sin and trespass offering was purification and forgiveness, the primary point of the burnt, meal and peace offering was to approach God with a *qorban* offering presented as incense to God.

As addressed in chapter two, the burnt, meal and peace offerings can be called "sweet savour offerings."[8] "Sweet savor" means a pleasing aroma or soothing fragrance. "Sweet savour" is a different Hebrew word than "incense" but it conveys the same idea. These "sweet savour" offerings were to be presented in the sense of burning incense to God.

Sweet savour offerings had two primary objects marked out by two dominant verbs: *qarab*, to approach God and *qatar*, to burn incense to God. Once we understand what incense symbolizes in the Bible, the true meaning of these sacrifices comes to light.

Incense Represents Prayer

In our culture, incense is often regarded as a nice but inefficient way to clear bad odors. However, in the Bible, incense represents prayer to God.

> Psalm 141:2:
> Let my prayer be set forth before thee *as* incense; *and* the lifting up of my hands *as* the evening sacrifice.

The literal translation from the Hebrew is, "Let my prayer be set before thee, incense…" Prayer is equated to incense.

> Revelation 5:8:
> And when he had taken the book, the four beasts *and* four and twenty elders fell down before the Lamb, having every one of them harps, and golden vials full of odours [incense], which are the prayers of saints.

The golden vials full of incense are the prayers of the saints. Again, incense is the symbol for prayer. Few symbols in Scripture are set forth more straightforwardly than this.

In light of incense representing prayer, this abundant use of *qatar*—to burn as incense—carries the underlying sense of prayer. Therefore, defining the two Hebrew verbs *qarab* and *qatar*, and grasping what incense represents, brings into focus the great underlying idea of the burnt, meal, and peace offerings—**approaching God in prayer**.

Approaching God in Prayer in the New Testament

> Hebrews 9:28 and 10:1:
> So Christ was once offered to bear the sins of many; and unto them that look for him shall he appear the second time without sin unto salvation.
> For the law having a **shadow** of good things to come, *and* not the very image of the things, can never with those **sacrifices** which they offered year by year continually make the comers thereunto perfect.

As covered in chapter one, the Old Testament law and sacrifices were a shadow outline, a silhouette, of that coming Messiah who would offer himself. The sacrifices under the Law were set up by God in anticipation of the true and perfect sacrifice of Jesus Christ. The "good things to come," which the sacrifices foreshadowed, were the coming Savior and his accomplishments. The approach by sacrifice of the Old Covenant believer was a "shadow" of our approach to God by the sacrifice of Jesus Christ.

How do the sweet savour offerings of Leviticus portray the good things to come of the New Covenant? How do we approach God in prayer in the New Testament?

> Ephesians 2:16-18:
> And that he might reconcile both unto God in one body **by the cross**, having slain the enmity thereby:
> And came and preached peace to you which were afar off, and to them that were nigh.
> For through him we both have access **by one Spirit** unto the Father.

These verses mention two aspects of our approach to God. First, our approach or reconciliation to God is by the cross. Christ, by his death on the cross, became our approach offering. Second, as verse 18 says, our approach to God is by the spirit, ". . .we both have access by one Spirit unto the Father." Our access to God is by the gift of holy spirit we have within. Our moment by moment entry into God's presence is facilitated by this spirit.

Ephesians 6:18 mentions that we are to approach God in prayer by the spirit:

> Praying always with all prayer and supplication in the Spirit, and watching thereunto with all perseverance and supplication for all saints.

In addition to "prayer and supplication in the Spirit," God also exhorts us to continue ". . .watching thereunto with all perseverance. . ." God's Word makes this a priority.

I Corinthians 14 defines "prayer in the spirit."

> I Corinthians 14:14 and 15:
> For if I pray in an *unknown* tongue, my spirit prayeth, but my understanding is unfruitful.
> What is it then? I will pray **with the spirit**, and I will pray **with the understanding** also: I will sing with the spirit, and I will sing with the understanding also.

I Corinthians says there are two ways to approach God in prayer under this New Covenant—with the spirit and with the understanding. Verse 14 says, when you pray with an unknown tongue, speaking in tongues, you have no understanding of the words spoken.

The chapter continues with more explanation on praying in the spirit which is speaking in tongues.

> I Corinthians 14:16-19:
> Else when thou shalt bless with the spirit, how shall he that occupieth the room of the unlearned say Amen at thy **giving of thanks**, seeing he understandeth not what thou sayest?
> For thou verily **givest thanks well**, but the other is not edified.
> I thank my God, I speak with tongues more than ye all:
> Yet in the church I had rather speak five words with my understanding, that *by my voice* I might teach others also, than ten thousand words in an *unknown* tongue.

Both verse 16 and verse 17 refer to speaking in tongues as giving thanks. Hebrews tells us how much God appreciates our giving of thanks.

> Hebrews 13:12-16:
> Wherefore Jesus also, that he might sanctify the people with his own blood, suffered without the gate.
> Let us go forth therefore unto him without the camp, bearing his reproach.
> For here have we no continuing city, but we seek one to come.
> By him therefore let us offer the sacrifice of praise to God continually, that is, the fruit of *our* lips giving thanks to his name.
> But to do good and to communicate forget not: for with such sacrifices God is well pleased.

The Word of God says we are to "offer the sacrifice of praise to God continually, that is, the fruit of our lips giving thanks to his name." Our *sacrifices* are not the fruits of the ground or the firstlings of our herds but the adoration of our hearts and the devotion of our lives.[9] The outward ceremonial acts of the Old Covenant anticipated the inward spiritual realities of the New Covenant. Now we can "bless with the spirit" and "give thanks well" by speaking in tongues (I Corinthians 14:16 and 17). Perfect praise is available to us because of Christ's perfect work.

These sacrifices of praise from the spirit were first presented to God on the Day of Pentecost, the birthday of the Church.

> Acts 2:1-4:
> And when the day of Pentecost was fully come, they were all with one accord in one place.
> And suddenly there came a sound from heaven as of a rushing mighty wind, and it filled all the house where they were sitting.
> And there appeared unto them cloven tongues like as of fire, and it sat upon each of them.
> And they were all filled with the Holy Ghost, and began to speak with other tongues, as the Spirit gave them utterance.

Speaking in tongues is not a minor manifestation of little importance. Here on the Day of Pentecost, all the fullness of what Christ accomplished on the cross was made available for the first time. On this remarkable day, the apostles offered to God the sacrifice of praise by way of holy spirit. They spoke in tongues.

This Day of Pentecost inaugurated a new beginning in approaching God. A few weeks before, Jesus had paid the ultimate price by laying down his life as the final and perfect sacrifice for all time. The sacrificial shadows and types of the Old Testament were fulfilled. On this Day of Pentecost recorded in Acts 2, God gave the gift of holy spirit to facilitate our moment by moment access to Him. What a full and complete salvation we have in Christ! What boundless resources we have at our disposal! At any time, in any place in the world, we can have access to God by speaking in tongues. We can walk into God's holy presence by prayer in the spirit.

As we have seen, the sacrificial system of the Old Covenant restored some small measure of approach and fellowship with God. However, it was merely a faint outline of the Messiah who was to come. These approach offerings looked forward to the coming of the greater, Jesus Christ. He would be the way of approach for God's people for all time by being the approach offering. This truth was in the mind of God when He set up these sacrifices by revelation to Moses. God foreknowing Christ, foreshadowed Christ in these sacrifices.

Once this great purpose of the Old Testament sacrifices becomes clear, whole sections of the New Testament become vivid with this truth. This will be explored in the next chapter. In tracking Christ and his work on our behalf through the Scriptures, this old adage is so often true: "The Old Testament is the New Testament concealed, and the New Testament is the Old Testament revealed."

Notes

1. Of the nineteen uses of *Polyptoton*, in nine of them, the words *qarab* and *qorban* are right next to each other in the Hebrew text, thus forming the expression, "approaching with an approach offering." Ten times *qarab* and *qorban* are used in the same phrase but not in immediate succession.

2. In verses three and ten, *qarab* and *qorban* do not occur in immediate succession in the Hebrew text. Rather, they are repeated in the same phrase to bring attention to the approach by repetition of *qarab* and *qorban*.

3. In a bizarre twist of archaic English word usage, the only offering in Leviticus 1-7 with **no meat** is the "meat offering." Since, in our current usage, "meat" means the flesh of an animal, this offering of Leviticus 2 will be rendered "meal offering."

4. *Jesus Christ, Our Promised Seed*, Wierwille (New Knoxville, OH: American Christian Press, 1980), xxx.

5. The precise English word for the Hebrew *qatar* is "cense." Cense means to burn incense in worship, from the French *encenser* and Latin *incendo* (to burn). Cense is used in a liturgical context. When a priest in some Orthodox churches burns incense in a vase or pan (censer) suspended by a chain, this is called censing. This is not to be confused with "census" or "censor" which are from the Latin, *censere* (to assess, whether in judgement or for taxes).

6. *Qetoreth* (Strong's # 7004) is the noun form of *qatar* (Strong's # 6999) and is translated "incense" 54 times in KJV. *Qatar* contrasts with these Hebrew words which simply mean "to burn:"
    a. *saraph,* Leviticus 4:12, 21.
    b. *baar,* Leviticus 6:12 (second "burn").
    c. *yaqad,* Leviticus 6:9, 13.

7. These three sources define *qatar:* to burn incense, to offer fragrance conveying the sense of producing a pleasing aroma, a sweet fragrance unto God.
Gesenius, *Hebrew and Chaldee Lexicon* (1847; Grand Rapids: MI: Baker, 1979).
William Wilson, *Old Testament Word Studies* (Grand Rapids: MI: Kregel, 1987).
Robert Young, *Analytical Concordance to the Bible* (1879, Grand Rapids: MI: Eerdmans, 1960), s.v. *qatar.*

8. Leviticus 1:9, 13, 17; 2:2, 9; 3:5, 16.

9. Arthur Pink, *An Exposition of Hebrews* (Grand Rapids: MI: Baker, 1954), 1209.

4

Jesus Christ: Our Approach Offering

As we have observed in the previous chapters, the New Testament Scripture reveals in vivid detail what the Old Testament revelation only foreshadows. To review, in the first seven chapters of Leviticus, much emphasis is placed on approaching God. This Old Testament approach forecasts the fullness of what the coming Messiah would accomplish on our behalf. The *qorban* offerings anticipated what the sacrifice of Christ would bring into full realization. Now we will examine how whole sections of the New Testament open up with this truth—Jesus Christ, our approach offering.

The reality that we have constant access to a living and loving God is an unending source of peace and joy. As we dwell on this open reception to God that Christ has accomplished, our fellowship with God will grow and blossom. As we understand our unobstructed access, we can learn to abide in His tranquil presence. As we lay our burdens, fears, and anxieties down at God's feet, we can enter in His rest and approach into quiet fellowship with Him.

Prosagōgē, Access by an Intermediary

> Romans 5:2:
> By whom also we have access [*prosagōgē*] by faith into this grace wherein we stand, and rejoice in hope of the glory of God.

> Ephesians 2:18:
> For through him we both have access [*prosagōgē*] by one Spirit unto the Father.

> Ephesians 3:12:
> In whom we have boldness and access [*prosagōgē*] with confidence by the faith of him.

The precision of the Greek word, *prosagōgē,* is stunning. Its meaning is not simply "access" but "access by an intermediary"—to gain entrée by a go-between. This word is often used of gaining entrance into the presence of a king by means of a mediator who secures the privilege of an interview with the sovereign.[1] One insightful commentary states, ". . .the idea is that of introduction to the presence-chamber of a monarch. The rendering "access" is inadequate, as it leaves out of sight that we do not come in our own strength but need an 'introducer'—Christ."[2]

The beauty of *prosagōgē* is how it fits so perfectly with the New Testament revelation. Our Lord Jesus Christ is our intermediary to God. We now have freedom of entry to our Heavenly Father's throne because of our Lord's introduction. By the approach offering of Jesus Christ we have gained entrance to God. Jesus Christ, as mediating and interceding high priest escorts us into the throne room of God Almighty.

Prosagōgē is often used in the *Septuagint*, the ancient Greek translation of the Old Testament. This word is frequently used in place of the Hebrew word, *qorban*. Bible scholar Charles Welch observes that there are 37 occurrences in Leviticus where the Greek *Septuagint* translates *qorban* as *prosagōgē*.[3] These uses of *qorban* as *prosagōgē* reinforce the idea that the *qorban* offerings of Leviticus were, in essence, approach offerings. Also, this sacrificial usage of the word *prosagōgē*, corresponds to the definition of "an access by an intermediary." The Old Testament sacrifices served as an intermediary to bring the believer to God just as Christ does in the New Testament.

> I Peter 3:18:
> For Christ also hath once suffered for sins, the just for the unjust, that he might bring [*prosagō*] us to God, being put to death in the flesh, but quickened by the Spirit.

Jesus Christ offered himself once, not many times, like the multiple and repeated sacrifices under the Old Covenant. As Hebrews 9:28 says, "So Christ was once offered to bear the sins of many. . ." Christ was the once and for all time sacrifice for mankind.

The sacrifice of the "just for the unjust" is the basic sacrificial principle: substitution. The innocent lays down his life for the guilty. That is to say, the innocent sacrifice dies on behalf of, in the place of, the guilty party.

"Might bring" is the Greek *prosagō,* the verb form of the noun *prosagōgē*. It means "to lead to or towards, to bring near."[4] Jesus Christ has brought us near to God. By him we have an escorted entry into the throne of grace. Again, the *Septuagint* has a notable use of the Greek verb *prosagō*.

The Hebrew word *qarab*, to bring, was translated directly into the Greek word *prosagō* in Leviticus 1:2; 3:1 and 7:16.

Now that we have handled this wonderful and elucidating Greek word, let us continue to search out the results of Jesus Christ's offering through the New Testament.

Brought Near

Ephesians chapter 2 further illuminates the accomplishment of Jesus Christ.

> Ephesians 2:11-13:
> Wherefore remember, that ye *being* in time past Gentiles in the flesh, who are called Uncircumcision by that which is called the Circumcision in the flesh made by hands;
> That at that time ye were without Christ, being **aliens** from the commonwealth of Israel, and **strangers** from the covenants of promise, having no hope, and without God in the world:
> But now in Christ Jesus ye who sometimes were far off are made nigh [near] by the blood of Christ.

We are brought near to God by the sacrifice of Christ. The "blood of Christ" refers to Christ's shed blood in his sacrificial death. The sacrifice of Christ has gained us an audience with God. This closeness and companionship with our Creator is an abundant source of quiet joy.

> Ephesians 2:14 and 15:
> For he is our peace, who hath made both one, and hath broken down the middle wall of partition *between us*;
> Having abolished in his flesh the enmity, *even* the law of commandments *contained* in ordinances; for to

make in himself of twain one new man, *so* making peace.

In Leviticus, the two primary components of an animal sacrifice were the flesh and the blood. Here in Ephesians, the accomplishments of both the blood and the flesh of Christ are spelled out.

In the blood of Jesus Christ, we have an approach to God (verse 13). In the sacrifice of verse 15, Jesus Christ "abolished in his flesh the enmity, *even* the law of commandments." He abolished the law. He voided it out. Like a contract that has been totally completed, fulfilled, and paid for, the law was nullified. If the law was still in effect, the status of we Gentiles would still be as "aliens" and "strangers" before God (verse 12). Leviticus 1:2 said, "Speak unto the children of Israel. . ." Any approach under the Law was applicable only to those within covenant nation of Israel (Exodus 12:48). The nullifying of the Law and the Old Covenant gave us Gentiles an open door of access to God. Jesus completely fulfilled and terminated the Law of Moses by his sacrifice on the cross. There is no little portion of the Old Testament law still left lurking around that you need to fulfil.

In that momentous sacrifice of Christ, every legal obstacle between God and man was removed. The demands of the Law were fulfilled. The curse of the Law was removed. The veil was rent; the middle wall of partition was broken down. All the enmity between God and the believer was abolished. Christ made peace. God could be approached without fear or guilt by the offering of Jesus Christ.

> Ephesians 2:16:
> And that he might reconcile both unto God in one body by the cross, having slain the enmity thereby [in himself]:

"Thereby" is more accurately translated "in himself." On the cross, Christ slew the enmity between God and us **in himself** because all the alienation dividing God and us was transferred to Christ. Then, when he died, all our enmity with God died with him.

The accomplishments of the sacrifice of Christ are colossal. We have full reconciliation to God by the offering of Christ on the tree at Calvary. When Christ, the perfect sacrifice was slain, all the enmity between God and man and between Judean and Gentile was slain with him. Hence, we have free access to our Heavenly Father.

> Ephesians 2:17 and 18:
> And came and preached peace to you which were afar off, and to them that were nigh.
> For through him we both have access [*prosagōgē*] by one Spirit unto the Father.

By the approach offering of Jesus Christ, we have gained entrance to God. Now, Jesus Christ as mediating and interceding high priest brings us into the throne room. Our gracious introduction into God's presence is by Christ's efforts on our behalf.

Verse 18 also says we have access to God "**by one spirit**." I Corinthians 12:8-10 details the "manifestation of the spirit." By operating these nine manifestations of God's gift of holy spirit, we facilitate our access to God in practice, in the here and now. Without the operation of these manifestations of the spirit, our discussion of these wonderful truths of Jesus Christ our approach offering remains largely academic.

> Ephesians 2:19-22:
> Now therefore ye are no more strangers and foreigners, but fellowcitizens with the saints, and of the household of God;
> And are built upon the foundation of the apostles and prophets, Jesus Christ himself being the chief corner *stone*;
> In whom all the building fitly framed together groweth unto an holy temple in the Lord:
> In whom ye also are builded together for an habitation of God through the Spirit.

This magnificent revelation in Ephesians presents the glorious approach we have to God through the sacrifice of Jesus Christ. The central truth of our access to God by Jesus Christ our approach offering is expressed in a variety of ways. It is like one magnificent diamond with many glistening facets.

In verse 13 we are made near by the blood of Christ.
In verse 14 Christ is our peace offering. (See Appendix B.)
In verse 15 the enmity between us and God is abolished by his flesh given in sacrifice.
In verse 16 we, both Jew and Gentile, are reconciled by his work on the cross.
In verse 18 we, both Jew and Gentile, have access.
In verse 19 we are no longer strangers and foreigners but fellowcitizens.
In verses 20 and 21 the Church is illustrated or symbolized by the Old Testament temple of Solomon, which held the holy of holies where God dwelt in glory.
Verse 22 gleams most vividly. Like the temple of Solomon where God dwelt, so we as the Body of Christ are a

habitation of God by way of holy spirit. In us, the Church, God dwells with all His glory.

In verse 20, the illustration of Christ switches. He is not referred to as an offering but as part of the temple—the "chief cornerstone."[5] The closing two verses of chapter two in Ephesians shift from the sacrificial illustration to temple imagery. The limits of what Christ has accomplished for us as represented by the approach offering have been reached.

The reality of our approach to God by Jesus Christ is simply too big to be limited to only the illustration of the offering. Understanding Jesus Christ as our approach offering clarifies <u>how</u> this approach occurred—an innocent sacrifice dies in our place to bring us to God. Shifting to different imagery—the temple—demonstrates the profound greatness of <u>what</u> occurred. God, by way of His gift of holy spirit, dwells in us just as the glory of God dwelt in the temple. As the glory of God dwelt in the holy of holies in the tabernacle of Moses and the temple of Solomon, so we have the fabulous reality of the spirit of God dwelling in us. Look at the utter magnitude of Christ's work. It is almost astonishing how far God has gone, through Christ, to bring us unto Himself.

This powerful and vivid imagery in Ephesians is not man's invention or device. It is God speaking to us, explaining the breadth and depth of all He has accomplished for us by Christ. These wonderful truths should transport our hearts to His peace and joy. The days of melancholy and depression are past. As we digest this manna of God's Word, we can revel and rejoice in the immensity of Christ's accomplishments.

The emphasis of this book is on Jesus Christ our approach offering. However, the reality of what his work accomplished is so profoundly extensive and consequential that the New Testament uses three primary illustrations from the Law to communicate the great access we have to God: the sacrifices, the high priest, and the tabernacle/temple. We will soon see that these remarkable illustrations are most thoroughly explained in Hebrews.

Regardless of how it is explained or symbolized, we have a personally escorted introduction into the presence of God by Christ. While Christ's death obtained our entrance unto the Father, our continuous moment-by-moment access to God is by the gift of holy spirit that He has given us. God's work on our behalf, through Christ, did not stop with his death. Our unhindered pathway to God was fully completed by Christ's resurrection, ascension and the giving of the holy spirit on the Day of Pentecost.

Jesus Christ, Our Approach Offering in Romans and Hebrews

There are two great lengthy doctrinal treatises in the New Testament revelation: Romans and Hebrews. Hebrews expresses New Testament realties in Old Covenant terminology. Romans uses broader terms, appealing to a more universal worldwide audience.

The momentous work of Jesus Christ, our approach offering, is explained in both Hebrews and Romans. While Hebrews is steeped in rich Levitical terminology, the teaching of Romans is often framed with illustrations of sonship, slavery, and law. In reference to our access to God, both Hebrews and Romans address this awesome truth. This is not to say that the Book of Romans is devoid of Old Testament terms or, indeed, that Hebrews does not have universal appeal. However, Romans being written to both Jew and Gentile believers (Romans 1:14-16), uses more general terms to express the momentous point of our approach to God by Jesus Christ's sacrifice. Romans has good reason to employ terms and illustrations more universally applicable to humanity in general. One of the functions of Romans is to lay the groundwork to reach out to the nations (Gentiles) and to explain how and why they share fully in Christ's redemptive work. In contrast, Hebrews' terms and illustrations explain Christ's work as rooted in the Old Covenant instituted under the Mosaic Law.

The equivalent truth of our approach to God by Christ in both Romans and Hebrews is seen when comparing these two sections of each book:

> Romans 8:31-39:
> What shall we then say to these things? If God *be* for us, who *can be* against us?
> He that spared not his own Son, but delivered him up for us all, how shall he not with him also freely give us all things?
> Who shall lay any thing to the charge of God's elect? *It is* God that justifieth.
> Who *is* he that condemneth? *It is* Christ that died, yea rather, that is risen again, who is even at the right hand of God, who also maketh intercession for us.
> Who shall separate us from the love of Christ? *shall* tribulation, or distress, or persecution, or famine, or nakedness, or peril, or sword?
> As it is written, For thy sake we are killed all the day long; we are accounted as sheep for the slaughter.

> Nay, in all these things we are more than conquerors through him that loved us.
> For I am persuaded, that neither death, nor life, nor angels, nor principalities, nor powers, nor things present, nor things to come,
> Nor height, nor depth, nor any other creature, shall be able to **separate us** from the love of God, which is in Christ Jesus our Lord.

This section of Romans closes with the grand issue of the ages. Who shall separate us? Who or what is able to wrench us from God? Now that Christ has come and finished his work of redemption and salvation, we have the right and the privilege to abide in God's presence. We have been reconciled. No force or power has the capacity to deprive us of our access into God's throne room. We are indeed more than conquerors through him, the Lord Jesus Christ, who loved us.

Now we are at the very crest of Romans—in the spiritual Himalayas of Biblical truth. We gaze in wonder at the spectacular view. One eminent truth stands at the pinnacle: nothing shall separate us; we have unhindered approach to God. While at this heavenly altitude, we can gaze off in the distance and see the sister peak which echoes the same truth:

> Hebrews 10:19-22:
> Having therefore, brethren, boldness to enter into the holiest by the blood of Jesus,
> By a new and living way, which he hath consecrated for us, through the veil, that is to say, his flesh;
> And *having* an high priest over the house of God;

Let us draw near with a true heart in full assurance of faith, having our hearts sprinkled from an evil conscience, and our bodies washed with pure water.

Just as Romans 8:37-39 sums up what has been previously stated in Romans, Hebrews 10:19-22 concludes ground covered in Hebrews. While Romans uses terms non-Judeans can understand, Hebrews renders these truths in the richly textured illustrations of the Old Testament Law—tabernacle, sacrifices, and high priest.

In this compressed summary of what has preceded, Hebrews 10:19-22 combines vivid imagery of tabernacle, sacrifices, and high priest:
Verse 19: the blood of Christ: by his sacrifice we have boldness to enter.
Verse 20: the veil of the holy of holies: through which we enter.
Verse 21: high priest: Jesus Christ is our high priest.

The Book of Romans fully expresses Christ as a sacrificial offering on our behalf. But its presentation is for a broader audience. Romans 8 says, ". . .spared not his own Son, but delivered him up for us all. . ." Christ died as a substitute, in our place. Romans is a masterpiece of universal truth, not requiring previous knowledge of the Mosaic Law.

> Romans 5:2-8:
> By whom also we have access [*prosagōgē*] by faith into this grace wherein we stand, and rejoice in hope of the glory of God.
> And not only *so*, but we glory in tribulations also: knowing that tribulation worketh patience;
> And patience, experience; and experience, hope:

> And hope maketh not ashamed; because the love of God is shed abroad in our hearts by the Holy Ghost which is given unto us.
> For when we were yet without strength, in due time Christ died for the ungodly.
> For scarcely for a righteous man will one die: yet peradventure for a good man some would even dare to die.
> But God commendeth his love toward us, in that, while we were yet sinners, Christ died for us.

Verses 6-8 contain one of the most poignant expressions ever written of one giving his life in substitution for another. This is the *King James Version* in all of its poetic eloquence: "For scarcely for a righteous man will one die: yet peradventure for a good man some would even dare to die." Our modern English translations are in linguistic poverty compared to the lyrical richness of the *King James*.[6]

Though it strains credulity, Christ gave his life for sinners—not for the righteous, not for the good, but for the ungodly. No matter what language this passage may be translated into, the message is clear. No previous knowledge of the Mosaic law is necessary. In strikingly beautiful yet simple prose, the basic principle of substitution is explained—the innocent lays down his life for the guilty.

> Romans 5:9-11:
> Much more then, being now justified by his blood, we shall be saved from wrath through him.
> For if, when we were enemies, we were reconciled to God by the death of his Son, much more, being reconciled, we shall be saved by his life.

> And not only *so*, but we also joy in God through our Lord Jesus Christ, by whom we have now received the atonement [reconciliation].

In the phrase, "we were reconciled to God by the death of his Son," again, while not stated in the Old Testament terminology of the approach offering, the same truth is conveyed.

Theme of Hebrews: Approaching God

The central theme of Hebrews is approaching God. Some scholars have called Hebrews a New Testament commentary on Leviticus. Indeed, Hebrews is much more. It bridges the Old and the New Testaments, showing how the three institutions set up by Moses—the priesthood, the tabernacle, and the sacrifices—serve to illustrate and foreshadow the coming Messiah. But our focus here is on the central theme of both Leviticus and Hebrews—approaching God.

Hebrews utilizes diverse terms and assorted illustrations to express this one central idea of approaching God. In Hebrews, the believer is repeatedly exhorted to "draw near," "enter in," and to "come unto." Hebrews 2:10 speaks of "bringing many sons unto glory" by the sacrificial death of Christ. God gives the "how and why" of coming before God's throne of grace in the book of Hebrews.

Old Testament history is used in chapters three and four to portray entering into God's rest. The deficient reaction of the Exodus generation to God's promise to enter into the Promised Land serves as an illustration to exhort the New Covenant believers to enter into God's rest and presence.

The Greek word for enter, *erchomoi*, is used an amazing eleven times in these two chapters.[7]

Chapter four closes with the sublime appeal to: "come boldly unto the throne of grace that we may obtain mercy, and find grace to help in time of need." The closing phrase could be rendered, ". . find grace to help at the right time."[8] The point here is that God's help is never late. His timing is impeccable. We should not give up in panic and bolt from God's fellowship right before His deliverance is manifested. We should instead exhibit the fidelity and tranquility of Shadrach, Meshach, and Abednego.

> Daniel 3:16-18:
> Shadrach, Meshach, and Abednego, answered and said to the king, O Nebuchadnezzar, we *are* not careful to answer thee in this matter.
> If it be *so*, our God whom we serve is able to deliver us from the burning fiery furnace, and he will deliver *us* out of thine hand, O king.
> But if not, be it known unto thee, O king, that we will not serve thy gods, nor worship the golden image which thou hast set up.

Perhaps you know the story. Although tossed into the huge fiery furnace, they were delivered—not a "hair of their head singed, neither were their coats changed, nor the smell of fire had passed on them" (Daniel 3:27). As they were being thrown into the furnace it may have seemed that their "time of need" had well passed. But the good pleasure of God's will in this situation far exceeded all human expectation. God's deliverance was not tardy.

The Book of Hebrews employs Old Testament geography in chapter twelve to illustrate our approach to God. Mount Sinai and Zion are compared to contrast the approach to

God in the Old Covenant and in the New. The dramatic sense of the unapproachable Mount Sinai is compared to the approach of God's people to the heavenly Jerusalem or Mount Zion. This illustration will be examined in detail in chapter 10.

One Greek word used in Hebrews that is fundamental to our study of Jesus Christ our approach offering, is *proserkomai*. Each time this word appears in Hebrews, it is used in the sacrificial or priestly sense. Thus, this word could be translated more literally as "approach." Many other English versions often render this word, *proserkomai*, accurately as "approach."[9]

Here is how *proserkomai* is used in Hebrews: (The English words translated from the Greek word are emphasized in bold print.)

4:16: **Let us** therefore **come** boldly **unto** the throne of grace. . .
7:25: . .he is able also to save them to the uttermost that **come unto** God by him. . .
10:1: . . can never with those sacrifices . . . make the **comers** there**unto** perfect.
10:22: **Let us draw near** with a true heart. . .
11:6: . . .for he that **cometh to** God must believe. . .
12:18: For ye are not **come unto** mount Sion. . .
12:22: But ye are **come unto** mount Sion. . .

In the next section we will look at some of these uses of *proserkomai*.

Jesus Christ as Intercessor in Romans and High Priest in Hebrews

While this book's focus is on Christ as our approach offering, Jesus Christ as our high priest warrants mention.

> Hebrews 7:23-25:
> And they truly were many priests, because they were not suffered to continue by reason of death:
> But this *man*, because he continueth ever, hath an unchangeable priesthood.
> Wherefore he is able also to save them to the uttermost that come unto [*proserkomai*] God by him, seeing he ever liveth to make intercession for them.

Jesus Christ, as our high priest, makes intercession for us. An integral part of our access to God is the function of Jesus Christ as our high priest. Again, comparing Romans and Hebrews yields the same results as before. Romans states the same truth but in more general terms not requiring an understanding of the Old Testament law.

> Romans 8:34:
> Who *is* he that condemneth? *It is* Christ that died, yea rather, that is risen again, who is even at the right hand of God, who also maketh intercession for us.

Jesus Christ is at the right hand of God, making intercession for us. This is exactly the role of Jesus Christ as our high priest. However, here it is stated only as intercessor—an idea that every Gentile can understand. From the most primitive tribe to the most intricate corporate bureaucracy, everyone grasps the concept and the value of a "go-between," or an intercessor. Romans, addressed to all cultures, in all parts of the globe, simply says, "intercession." On the other hand, Hebrews explains, in exquisite detail, the parallels between Christ as our high priest and the Old Testament high priest.

Believing to Approach God in Romans and Hebrews

Another similarity between Romans and Hebrews is that both books place compelling emphasis on believing to approach God. Access to God is to be accompanied with believing.

> Romans 5:2:
> By whom also we have access [*prosagoge*] by faith into this grace wherein we stand, and rejoice in hope of the glory of God.

Our access to God is by believing.

> Hebrews 10:22:
> Let us draw near [*proserkomai*] with a true heart in full assurance of faith, having our hearts sprinkled from an evil conscience, and our bodies washed with pure water.

We are to approach with a true heart in full certainty.

> Hebrews 11:6:
> But without faith *it is* impossible to please *him*: for he that cometh to [*proserkomai*] God must believe that he is, and *that* he is a rewarder of them that diligently seek him.

Just as with Romans, the cardinal practical key to appropriating our approach into God's divine presence is believing. The closing statement of Romans 8 begins with the words, "For I am persuaded. . ." Speaking of the believing of Abraham, Romans says, "being fully persuaded that, what he had promised, he was able also to perform."(Romans 4:21). Our response to what God has done in Christ, whether stated in Romans or Hebrews, is identical. We are to believe what God has spoken to us in His Word.

An intellectual appreciation is not enough. The realization of access into God's very presence must sink into the depths of our hearts. Then we can approach God, to stand before Him and make our requests known.

"I am the Door"

In the Gospel of John, Jesus states with simple elegance that he is the door into God's presence.

> John 10:1-17:
> Verily, verily, I say unto you, He that entereth not by the door into the sheepfold, but climbeth up some other way, the same is a thief and a robber.
> But he that entereth in by the door is the shepherd of the sheep.
> To him the porter openeth; and the sheep hear his voice: and he calleth his own sheep by name, and leadeth them out.
> And when he putteth forth his own sheep, he goeth before them, and the sheep follow him: for they know his voice.
> And a stranger will they not follow, but will flee from him: for they know not the voice of strangers.
> This parable spake Jesus unto them: but they understood not what things they were which he spake unto them.

Then said Jesus unto them again, Verily, verily, I say unto you, **I am the door of the sheep.**
All that ever came before me are thieves and robbers: but the sheep did not hear them.
I am the door: by me if any man enter in, he shall be saved, and shall go in and out, and find pasture.
The thief cometh not, but for to steal, and to kill, and to destroy: I am come that they might have life, and that they might have *it* more abundantly.
I am the good shepherd: the good shepherd giveth his life for the sheep.
But he that is an hireling, and not the shepherd, whose own the sheep are not, seeth the wolf coming, and leaveth the sheep, and fleeth: and the wolf catcheth them, and scattereth the sheep.
The hireling fleeth, because he is an hireling, and careth not for the sheep.
I am the good shepherd, and know my *sheep*, and am known of mine.
As the Father knoweth me, even so know I the Father: and I lay down my life for the sheep.
And other sheep I have, which are not of this fold: them also I must bring, and they shall hear my voice; and there shall be one fold, *and* one shepherd.
Therefore doth my Father love me, because I lay down my life, that I might take it again.

In the ancient eastern cultures the shepherd would sleep in the door of the sheepfold to protect the sheep.[10] In this picturesque extended metaphor Jesus is the door of the sheepfold. In this passage Jesus is the shepherd who is the door. This is one illustration of Christ, not two.

In verse nine, the point of this parable[11] is made clear: **I am the door: by me if any man enter in, he shall be saved.** The point of entrée is Christ. He is the entrance, the door. But this shepherd lays down his life for the sheep. Our true shepherd, the Lord Jesus Christ, gives his life for God's people:
Verse 11: ". . .I am the good shepherd: the good shepherd giveth his life for the sheep.
Verse 15: ". . .I lay down my life for the sheep."
Verse 17: ". . .I lay down my life. . ."

As we have seen so abundantly elsewhere in Scripture, in laying down his life, Jesus Christ became God's approach offering for all people for all time. For this reason, he is the door, God's entry way to Himself. He is the portal into God's presence.

"I am the Way"

> John 14:6:
> Jesus saith unto him, I am the way, the truth, and the life: no man cometh [approaches] unto the Father, but by me.

Jesus Christ is the way, the approach to God. There is no admittance, no entrée to God, without him. But why is Jesus Christ the only way to God? Because he is the **only** approach offering.

Some say it is the height of arrogance to say Jesus Christ is the only way to God. So, let's give some of humanities greatest religious leaders the benefit of the doubt. Buddha, Mohammed, and Gandhi had some profound ideas. Their teaching and influence brought people some measure of relief from darkness and oppression. Helpful as they may have been, they were not, nor ever claimed to be, an approach offering for God's people. They did not lay down their lives fulfilling Old Testament prophecies of the coming Messiah. None of them were raised from the dead. None of them ever did what Jesus Christ did—lay down his life as an approach offering and then rise from the dead.

From the fall of Adam and Eve in Genesis 3, there was no approach to God without a sacrifice. Jesus Christ paid the price required. He laid down his life as an offering for us. Jesus Christ is the only approach to God because he is the only approach offering.

People may claim, "I have the best belief system—it will bring me to God. By focusing my thoughts, I bring God and His energy to me." You do not bring God to you. You can only approach Him through the approach offering, Jesus Christ. There is no entrance to God without an approach offering.

Others claim, "my religious affiliation will bring me to God—I got baptized in the church." Your affiliation, religious or otherwise, may bring you beneficial contacts in life, but it will not bring you to God. The only approach to God is by the approach offering He has provided, the Lord Jesus Christ.

> Hebrews 10:19 and 20:
> Having therefore, brethren, boldness to enter into the holiest by the blood of Jesus,
> By a new [freshly slain] and living way, which he hath consecrated [inaugurated, initiated] for us, through the veil, that is to say, his flesh;

Jesus Christ opened the way to God for us by the sacrifice of himself. His sacrifice was the inauguration of a new age of access to God for the believer.

Notes

1. This word is only used 3 times in the New Testament. Joseph Henry Thayer, *Greek-English Lexicon of New Testament* (Milford: MI: Baker, 1977), 543.
Gerhard Kittel, *Theological Dictionary of the New Testament* (Grand Rapids: MI: Eerdmans, 1967), Volume 1, 134.
Liddell & Scott's New Testament Lexicon (London: Oxford: Clarendon Press, 1975), 685. s.v. *prosagōgē*.

2. From *The International Critical Commentary* (1895) on Romans 5:2; quoted in *Kittels*, Volume 1, 134.

3. Charles H. Welch, *In Heavenly Places* (London: Berean Publishing Trust), 248.

4. E. W. Bullinger, *Critical Lexicon* (London: Bagster, 1974), 114. s.v. bring, *prosagō*.

5. This metaphor of Christ as the "cornerstone" can be a reference to Isaiah 28:16, referring to the large foundation stones of the temple at Jerusalem. Or the cornerstone could refer to a copestone, the giant stone that caps the tops of the pillars. "Chief," the adjective modifying "cornerstone," is the Greek word *akron* meaning top, the highest or furthest point (*Lindell & Scott's*, 30). See Luke 16:24 and Hebrews 11:21 for uses of *akron*.

6. See Adam Nicolson, *God's Secretaries: the Making of the King James Bible* (New York: Harper Collins, 2003). He says the KJV combines linguistic creativeness, and

bubbling vitality with an iron frame of fidelity to the original text.

7. Also in John 10:1, 2, 9 and twice and in Revelation 22:14.

8. Craig R. Koester, *The Anchor Bible, Hebrews* (New York: Doubleday, 2001), 285.

9. *The New American Bible* and the *New Revised Standard Version* are the most consistent and accurate, rendering most uses of *proserkomai* as "approach" in the Book of Hebrews.

10. K. C. Pillai, "The Shepherds," *The Way Magazine* (April 1965), 12.

11. Actually the Greek word for "parable" is *paroimia*, usually translated "figure of speech" (NIV, NAB, NAS). Bullinger's *Figures of Speech* classifies John 10:9 as a metaphor.

5

The Veil Rent
"There is Nothing more that I can do, Jesus Paid it all"

The Book of Hebrews is of supreme value in explaining how the Old Testament foreshadows Christ. In this sense, Hebrews forms a bridge from the Old to the New. In Hebrews, God clearly shows how three institutions that Moses set up by divine revelation—the priesthood, the tabernacle, and the sacrifices—serve to illustrate and foreshadow the coming Messiah.

At the moment of Christ's death on the cross, God rent the veil of the temple. This rending of the veil was a most dramatic demonstration that Jesus Christ was the ultimate approach offering to bring us to God. The rending of the veil signaled the absolute fulfillment and termination of the three great institutions set up by Moses—the high priest, the tabernacle, and the sacrifices.[1] With the veil torn asunder, the exclusivity of the priestly approach was gone. The temple veil rent asunder demonstrated that all of the approach offerings instituted in Leviticus were now of none effect. The way was open into God's presence by the sacrifice of Christ alone. And most dramatically, the tearing of the veil in two, from top to bottom, indicated that the tabernacle originally set up by Moses was no longer valid. How could God be more graphic?

> Matthew 27:50 and 51:
> Jesus, when he had cried again with a loud voice, yielded up the ghost.
> And, behold, the veil of the temple was rent in twain from the top to the bottom; and the earth did quake, and the rocks rent;

When Jesus Christ died, the veil of the temple was rent in two. Luke 23:45 adds that it was "rent in the midst." It was not rent off on the side but right down the middle. In his book, *The Tabernacle*, Henry Soltau explains:

> The vail hung upon four pillars; and the ark was placed in the centre of the holiest [holy of holies]; so that, the vail being rent in the midst, from top to bottom, a way of approach was made *directly* to the very centre of the mercy-seat, where, between the cherubim, the God of glory dwelt. It was not a *side* access, but the shortest and most direct that could be made, to the fore-front of the ark.[2]

Rending the veil was no small feat. The historian Edersheim says that the veil before the holy of holies was 60 feet long, 30 feet wide, and the thickness of the palm of one's hand.[3]

In Hebrews, the significance of the rent veil is explained in detail. Hebrews chapter nine reviews the basics of how Moses set up the tabernacle in Exodus.

> Hebrews 9:1-3:
> Then verily the first *covenant* had also ordinances of divine service, and a worldly sanctuary.
> For there was a tabernacle made; the first [room], wherein *was* the candlestick, and the table, and the

shewbread; which is called the sanctuary [the holy place].
And after the second veil, the tabernacle which is called the Holiest of all [holy of holies];

The Tabernacle had two different rooms. The first room was called "the holy place" or, here in verse two, it is called the "sanctuary." The "second veil" separated the holy place from the **most** holy place or "holy of holies." The Greek for "the holiest of all" is *hagia hagion,* more literally translated as "the holy of holies." This second room was the holy of holies where the high priest could only go in alone, once a year, on the Day of Atonement.

Verse 4-6:
Which had the golden censer, and the ark of the covenant overlaid round about with gold, wherein *was* the golden pot that had manna, and Aaron's rod that budded, and the tables of the covenant;
And over it the cherubims of glory shadowing the mercyseat; of which we cannot now speak particularly.
Now when these things were thus ordained, the priests went always into the first [room of the] tabernacle, accomplishing the service *of God.*

The "first tabernacle" is referring to the first room of the tabernacle, the holy place, wherein the priests went frequently to carry out the services.

Hebrews 9:7 and 8:
But into the second [holy of holies] *went* the high priest **alone once every year**, not without blood, which he offered for himself, and *for* the errors of the people:

> The Holy Ghost this signifying, that **the way** into the holiest of all [holy of holies] was not yet made manifest, while as the first tabernacle was yet standing.

God, the Holy Spirit, signified that the way into His most holy place was not yet open under the Mosaic tabernacle. The high priest was allowed access to the holy of holies only one day a year, on the Day of Atonement (as explained in Leviticus 16). By this annual ritual, God communicated that the way into His very presence was not yet manifest. The high priest's unaccompanied yearly entry on the Day of Atonement was a visual demonstration that access to God was highly restricted under the Old Covenant. Christ, The Way into God's holy presence, had not yet come.

The words, **"alone once,"** in verse seven, thunder off the page! God's people were barred from the very presence of God. This was so contrary to God's ultimate desire because God's will is to be with His people. God has the heart of a father. As a father, God wants His children to be near to Him. He wants to be surrounded by His people, to commune and fellowship. God wants to be a part of our daily lives.

As a father myself, I enjoy the time spent with my children. I take pleasure in seeing their unique talents and abilities develop. I love their distinct and delightful personalities. I enjoy helping them with guidance on how to manage situations they face. When my college age kids are gone for a few weeks or even a few days, I want to spend time with them and hear how they are doing. Would our Heavenly Father, who gave His Son for us, want any less than the relationship I have with my children?

God's heart must have ached from having been shut off and segregated from His people under the Old Covenant. However, God had a purpose. God had a plan. He patiently looked forward to the coming Christ. As both priest and offering, Christ would open the way into God's presence. Then the restricted access to God would end.

God intended the high priest's entrance into the holy of holies to foreshadow Christ's work. The high priest would enter once a year and intercede for the people. The Old Testament high priest foreshadowed Christ who would ascend into the most holy sanctum of heaven after his resurrection. There, in the presence of God, the Lord Jesus Christ would start his great ministry of intercession for God's people.

> Hebrews 7:25:
> Wherefore he is able also to save them to the uttermost that come unto God by him, seeing he ever liveth to make intercession for them.

To this day, Christ continues to exercise his priestly office on our behalf. He is our mediator, our advocate. He is actively interceding for us at the right hand of God.[4] We have a high priest over the house of God (Hebrews 10:21). What grace and glory we should manifest in our lives!

Our Entry through the Veil

> Hebrews 10:19-21:
> Having therefore, brethren, boldness to enter into the holiest by the **blood** of Jesus,
> By a new [newly slain, freshly slaughtered] and living way, which he hath consecrated [inaugurated, initiated] for us, through the veil, that is to say, his **flesh**;

And *having* an high priest over the house of God;

Verse 20 speaks of Christ's flesh given in sacrifice, while verse 19 refers to his blood. We approach God by both the blood and by the flesh of Jesus Christ's sacrifice. Both the blood and the flesh facilitated our entrance into God's presence.

The two basic elements of all sacrifice are blood and flesh. In the Old Testament ordinances about animal sacrifices, both the blood and the flesh were emphasized. In Leviticus, where the procedures concerning sacrifices are explained, the blood and the flesh are of prime concern and significance.

The meal offering, where no blood was shed, was usually paired with a drink offering of wine (Numbers 28). The meal offering coupled with the drink offering represented the flesh and the blood of sacrifice. This joint sacrifice was a precursor to the bread and wine of the holy communion. Therefore, in both the Old Testament and the New, special and separate emphasis is put on each element of sacrifice—the blood and the flesh.

As stated in Hebrews 10:19 and 20, both elements of Christ's sacrifice purchased our boldness to enter God's presence. Both the flesh and the blood of our Lord were offered on our behalf so we could approach God freely. Jesus Christ is our approach offering. He is the new and living way into God's presence.[5]

Hebrews 10:20 begins as follows: "By a new and living way. . ." The Greek word for "new" is *prosphatos,* which is made up of *pros* meaning recently or newly, and *phatos* meaning slain or slaughtered. Christ is both newly slain <u>and</u> living. What a striking contrast that should alert our minds to this outstanding truth!⁶ The "newly slain" refers to the crucifixion. The "living" refers to the resurrection. Death is the antithesis of life, yet God uses both—Christ's death and resurrection—in synergy to obtain our full access to Him. Christ as newly slain <u>in his death</u> and living <u>in his resurrection</u> is the only way into God's presence.

Verse 20 continues: ". . .Which he hath consecrated [inaugurated, initiated] for us, through the veil, that is to say, his flesh;" Jesus has initiated a new and living way to God for us. This profound truth can only be understood in light of the rent veil of Matthew 27:51. Our approach into God's presence is through the veil being completely torn in half.

But here in Hebrews 10:20 a deeper truth is added: ". . .the veil, that is to say, his flesh." The flesh of Christ, given in sacrifice, is equated to and symbolized by the veil of the temple. When God tore the veil in half at the moment of our Savior's death, He expressed three fabulous truths. First, the rending of the veil in half represented the sacrificial death of Christ. Second, it demonstrated that access to God had been accomplished—the way was opened. And third, the veil torn down the center symbolized the establishment of the New Covenant.

1. <u>The rending of the veil represents the death of Christ</u>. Here in Hebrews, it states the veil of the temple represented the flesh of Christ: ". . .the veil, that is to say, his flesh." At the exact moment of Christ's death, the veil was ripped down the middle. The rending of the veil symbolized the rending of Christ's flesh, his death.

2. <u>The rending of the veil represents our access to God</u>. This veil separated God from man. Now that Christ had laid down his life as the ultimate once-and-for-all-time

sacrifice, the way was open into God's presence. Previously only an ordained high priest of the line of Aaron could enter in once a year. But now every believer has a direct approach to God through Christ. Jesus Christ is now **the way** through the veil into the holy of holies, God's presence.

The flesh of Jesus Christ had to be "rent," that is, he had to die before the way into God's presence could be inaugurated. Hence, at the point of his death God ripped the veil in two, thus symbolizing that the ultimate approach offering had been slain. All obstacles to God were removed. All the blockage and the debris of sin, between God and His people, had been taken away.

3. <u>The rending of the veil represents the establishment of the New Covenant</u>. Again, please look at Hebrews 10:19 and 20:

> Having therefore, brethren, boldness to enter into the holiest by the blood of Jesus,
> By a new and living way, which he hath consecrated for us, through the veil, that is to say, his flesh;

Consider the picture presented here in light of Matthew 27:51. Hebrews portrays the saints as entering in <u>through the veil</u>. Then a most unusual statement is made—". . .the veil, that is to say, his flesh." The veil, rent in two from to top to bottom, is equated to Christ's flesh.

This imagery suggests that Christ's flesh was rent, and we have passed through it to the holy of holies. Remember, the veil of the temple was not partially torn, pierced or merely damaged; it was completely torn from top to bottom, completely separated. So the picture presented here is that we pass in between the two rent parts of the veil into God's presence. To equate the flesh of Christ with the veil, as this verse does, suggests that symbolically we pass through Christ's rent flesh in the same manner. The way to God is through the rent veil, the flesh of Christ.

Although this imagery is extremely unusual and perplexing to the modern mind, it has been used before in the Scriptures as a form of covenant making. In Bible times, to rend a newly slain sacrifice and pass between the two parts was a means of making a covenant.

> Jeremiah 34:18:
> And I will give the men that have transgressed my covenant, which have not performed the words of the covenant which they had made before me, when they cut the calf in twain [two], and passed between the parts thereof.

In Jeremiah, a covenant is made by cutting a sacrifice in two and walking between the parts. In Genesis 15 God made a covenant with Abram in which this same procedure was performed.

> Genesis 15:17, 18a:
> And it came to pass, that, when the sun went down, and it was dark, behold a smoking furnace, and a burning lamp that passed between those pieces.
> In the same day the Lord made a covenant with Abram...

In Genesis, the burning lamp represents the presence of God. In this particular instance, God passed between the two pieces of the sacrifice. Passing between two pieces of a sacrifice signified a most solemn and binding covenant.[7]

Picture this illustration in Hebrews 10:19 and 20. You are entering into the Holy of Holiest, into God's presence. What do you have to pass through to enter in? You walk in between the two rent pieces of the veil. Then, in addition to this, God says this veil represents the flesh of Christ. You are passing in between the newly sacrificed flesh of Christ. While this ancient custom seems bizarre to the modern reader, it was nevertheless a very old form of covenant making.

The Salt Covenant

Another way of making a covenant in the ancient world was with salt. The salt covenant was an integral part of the Old Testament sacrifices

> Leviticus 2:13:
> And every oblation [*qorban,* approach offering] of thy meat offering shalt thou season with **salt**; neither shalt thou suffer the **salt of the covenant** of thy God to be lacking from thy meat offering: with **all thine offerings** [*qorban*] thou shalt offer [*qarab*] **salt**.

All the *qorban* offerings were to be offered with salt. The addition of salt to the offerings indicated a solemn covenant with God. Numbers 18:19 is also an example of this ancient covenant of salt.

> Numbers 18:19:
> All the heave offerings of the holy things, which the children of Israel offer unto the LORD, have I given thee, and thy sons and thy daughters with thee, by a statute for ever: it *is* a covenant of salt for ever before the LORD unto thee and to thy seed with thee.

Adding salt to offerings was a form of covenant making. Each time these salted offerings were offered, the salt covenant was once again made with God. A covenant of salt indicated a lifelong promise of loyalty. These offerings were to be made with a heart of commitment and dedication to God.[8]

Remarkably, the animal *qorban* sacrifices in the Old Testament involved all of these three ingredients: <u>death of the sacrifice, access to God, and covenant making</u>. Look at the detailed depiction these offerings gave of the coming Christ! More remarkably, consider the utter completeness of our Savior's work on our behalf. Christ wholly fulfilled the function of the sacrifices for purification of sin and approach to God. He now fulfils the role of the high priest before God so we may approach. Christ is presently **seated** in the true tabernacle of God, in the heavenlies, interceding on our behalf. Unlike Christ, the Old Testament priests never sat down. There was no seat in the Mosaic tabernacle! The Old Testament priest's work was never done and it never was completed.

> Hebrews 10:11 and 12:
> And every priest standeth daily ministering and offering oftentimes the same sacrifices, which can never take away sins:
> But this man, after he had offered one sacrifice for sins for ever, sat down on the right hand of God;

The Old Testament priests never sat down as they ministered in the tabernacle. Their work was never finished. But at the ascension, our Lord and Savior sat down, indicating his work was fully completed.

Hebrews 10:14:
For by one offering he hath perfected for ever them that are sanctified.

"Perfected" means to bring into a state of completion. Christ's work is complete; so, we are complete. Jesus Christ is a complete Savior. The salvation he accomplished for us was absolutely perfect and all encompassing. He left nothing undone.

As the old hymn says, "There is nothing more that I can do, Jesus paid it all; And I am complete in Him." What a Savior! What a salvation!

Notes

1. Jesus said, referring to the law and prophets, ". . .I am not come to destroy, but to fulfil" (Matthew 5:17). Christ did not destroy—*kataluō*—the law (Matthew 5:17). But he did abolish—*katargeō*—the law (II Corinthians 3:13). *Kataluō* means "utterly destroy." *Katargeō* means to reduce to inactivity, of none effect, render ineffective, inoperative or inactive. In our times, when the terms of a contract are fulfilled and the bill is paid in full, the contract is terminated. However, it is not "destroyed." W. E. Vine, *Vine's Expository Dictionary of New Testament Words* (McLean: Virginia, MacDonald), 15 and 16.

2. Henry Soltau, *The Tabernacle, The Priesthood and the Offerings* (Grand Rapids, MI, Kregel reprint 1972), 32. Leviticus 4:6, 17 says blood was sprinkled "before" the veil. Jewish tradition held that blood from sacrifices was on the veil from this sprinkling procedure. (*Joma* 5, 4). The veil would have been coated with the dried blood of the sacrifices. This deepens the illustration of the veil of the temple equating the flesh of Christ in sacrifice. This veil also contained the blood of the sacrifices—which also represented Christ's sacrifice!

3. Edersheim, *The Life and Times of Jesus the Messiah*, Volume II. (New York: Longmans, 1901), 611.

4. In E. W. Bullinger's *Lexicon,* the Greek word for "intercession" is wonderfully defined: "a falling in with, a meeting with, coming together; access, audience, intercourse; a petition; then, intercession; request

concerning others and on their behalf." With Christ at God's right hand, we have access and audience with God.

5. The blood of Christ and the flesh of Christ must remain, and be understood, in a sacrificial context. The flesh of Christ in Hebrews 10:22 simply and literally means his earthly body. (Also see Ephesians 2:13-16 and Colossians 1:20-22.)

Some confusion arises because, in the New Testament, "flesh" at times refers to the old man nature or sin nature. However, this cannot be applied to the "flesh of Christ" in its New Testament usage. Often the "flesh of Christ" is understood to mean Christ's "humanity" or his "human nature." This tends toward confusion. Here in Hebrews 10:20 the flesh of Christ is simply and clearly his physical body given in sacrifice. The types and the prophecies of Christ's flesh given in sacrifice in the Old Testament should remove any doubt in this matter. The most prominent example is Isaiah 53 referring to the flesh or physical body of the coming Messiah, <u>not</u> his "humanity" or "human nature."

Still, many eminent scholars appear to differ with my conclusion here, among them, Bullinger, Pink and Wuest. Perhaps they labored under the dark shadow of the multiple heresies and controversies of the 5-7th centuries of the Church where the "two natures of Christ" were fought over. Philip Sahaff in his *History of the Christian Church, Volume III* (page 708) enumerates five different controversies over the divine and the human nature of Christ. All this commotion missed the preeminent truth of Christianity: ". . .we are sanctified through the offering of the body of Jesus Christ once *for all*" (Hebrews 10:10).

6. *Figures of Speech Used in the Bible* by E. W. Bullinger explains this figure as *Antithesis* or Contrast on page 715. This figure contrasting death and life also occurs in Romans 6.

Scholars of rhetoric are aware of and teach this figure of speech, *Antithesis*. For example, Dr. David Zarefshy, a nationally recognized authority on rhetoric, gives examples from the JFK inaugural, of the figure of speech, *Antithesis*. ("Argumentation: The Study of Effective Reasoning," Lecture 20, The Teaching Company. 2001.) Scholars of rhetoric in our universities recognize these figures of speech and regard E. W. Bullinger's *Figures of Speech Used in the Bible* to be of great value. Yet sadly, until recently, Bible scholars and Christians ignored this whole field for the most part.

7. Chris Geer, "The Friend of God: An Introductory Study of Abraham; An Introductory Consideration of Biblical Covenants," *Future Considerations*, Issue 52 (January 1994): 6 and 7.

8. K. C. Pillai, *Light through an Eastern Window* (New York: Robert Speller, 1976), 24.

In light of our study this reference in Mark 9:49 becomes clear: ". . .every sacrifice shall be salted with salt." (However, the Nestle and the Tischendorf texts omit this phrase.)

6

Our Right of Boldness in Approaching God

To grasp the scope and size of our salvation and redemption is a lifelong project. God rent the veil of the temple at the crucifixion to graphically demonstrate our open approach unto Him. However, the breadth of our salvation and redemption in Christ extends to include not only our approach to God but the exact manner of that approach. Understanding our access to God with boldness adds another dimension to Christ's work and to our walks with God in this world.

> Hebrews 10:11-22:
> And every priest standeth daily ministering and offering oftentimes the same sacrifices, which can never take away sins:
> But this man, after he had offered one sacrifice for sins for ever, sat down on the right hand of God;
> From henceforth expecting till his enemies be made his footstool.
> For by one offering he hath perfected for ever them that are sanctified.
> *Whereof* the Holy Ghost also is a witness to us: for after that he had said before,
> This is the covenant that I will make with them after those days, saith the Lord, I will put my laws into their hearts, and in their minds will I write them;

> And their sins and iniquities will I remember no more.
> Now where remission of these *is, there is* no more offering for sin.
> **Having therefore, brethren, boldness [*parrhēsia*] to enter** into the holiest by the blood of Jesus,
> By a new and living way, which he hath consecrated for us, through the veil, that is to say, his flesh;
> And *having* an high priest over the house of God;
> **Let us draw near with a true heart in full assurance of faith**, having our hearts sprinkled from an evil conscience, and our bodies washed with pure water.

These spectacular verses encapsulate so much of what Christ has accomplished for us. They also serve to illuminate what has previously transpired in the Book of Hebrews. Our study in this chapter will revolve around the truths highlighted here in verses 19 and 22: the boldness we have in Christ and then how to utilize this boldness in approaching God. We will first define this boldness and then consider how to use it. Our bold approach to God is available now but we must be taught how to apply it.

Our Accomplished Boldness

> Hebrews 10:19:
> Having [*echō*] therefore, brethren, boldness [*parrhēsia*] to enter into the holiest by the blood of Jesus,

The Greek word used to describe our means of approach is *parrhēsia,* usually translated as "boldness." This word means "fearless candor, freedom of speech." This word also connotes plainness of speech, outspokenness, absence of fear in speaking. Wuest says that *"parrhēsia* is a compound of *pan,* 'all,' and *hrema,* 'speech'—literally—'all speech'. Its dominant idea is one of the boldness and confidence which are exhibited in freedom of speech, the unreserved, unfettered flow of language which is opposed to fear, ambiguity and reserve."[1] (See Appendix A.)

As we saw in the last chapter, the veil is rent. All obstacles between us and God have been taken away. The impediments between God and us have been swept aside by Christ's work. We now need to walk into the throne room of God with boldness. Let's get rid of the "veils" in our heart and life that keep us from God. There is no curtain, no veil, between us and God! It is available for every Christian to have an open and fruitful relationship with God.

Hebrews 10:19 refers to us "having" boldness. This is more than an exhortation to boldness. The verse is saying that this boldness has already been accomplished for us. In the past, I understood this verse as an exhortation to boldness, as the attitude to use in approaching God. However, upon closer examination of these references, it does not speak of a psychological mindset. Rather, it refers to a boldness that has been achieved for us in the sacrifice of Christ. This boldness is our right and privilege as sons of God. In Hebrews 10:19 the word for "having" is the Greek verb, *echō*, which implies a present, continued having or lasting possession.[2]

The following verses also use this form of the verb, *echō*, referring to something we <u>already</u> have:

> II Corinthians 4:13: We having [*echō*] the same spirit of faith. . .

> II Corinthians 7:1: Having [*echō*] therefore these promises...
>
> II Corinthians 3:12: Seeing then that we have [*echō*] such hope, we use great plainness [*parrhēsia*] of speech:

In these verses *echō* refers to that which has been accomplished for us by God in Christ. We already have the spirit; we already have the promises; we already have the hope. II Corinthians 3:12 says, since "we have such hope" we utilize great boldness and plainness in speaking God's Word.

In I John 5:14 this boldness is also expressed in terms of something we have:

> I John 5:14 and 15:
> And this is the confidence [*parrhēsia*] that we have [*echō*] in him, that, if we ask any thing according to his will, he heareth us:
> And if we know that he hear us, whatsoever we ask, we know that we have the petitions that we desired of him.

We have this boldness in him—in Christ—by his work of redemption he achieved for us. Now, in our prayer life, we should utilize it. Verse 15 states one of the essential keys to utilizing our accomplished boldness: "if we know that he hear us, whatsoever we ask, we know that we have the petitions..."

As in Hebrews 10:19 and I John 5:14, Ephesians also refers to our boldness as something we already have by Christ's accomplished work.

Ephesians 3:12:
In whom [Christ] we have boldness [*parrhēsia*] and access with confidence by the faith of him.

There is a remarkable construction and usage of the article "the" in the Greek text of Ephesians 3:12. The Greek more literally reads, ". . .we have **the** boldness and **the** access with confidence by **the** faith of him."

In Greek, when the article "the" is placed before an abstract noun, it gives the word greater force and points out the special "distinctness of the noun."[3] This is not just any boldness or just any access. This is not boldness or access in general. This is specifically **the** boldness and **the** access that Christ has achieved for us as defined in God's Word. Approaching God with fear and groveling is one way we could come before God. But it is not **the** special and distinct access we have in Christ. We could come before God like a cringing, whipped dog, but such an approach is not **the** right way of access or boldness.

We have this remarkable boldness and access with confidence "by **the** faith of him." Here, as with "the boldness" and "the access," the definite article is used with faith to draw attention to this word.[4] "**The** faith" in Ephesians 3:12 is not just faith or believing in a general sense, but it points forcefully to the special and distinct believing concerning our Lord Jesus Christ.[5]

In discussing "by the faith of him," we are brought to the point of this book; the entire purpose of this work is to explain Christ and contribute to building the believing concerning our access and boldness. Our goal is to expand beyond a general believing in Christ as our Savior to specifically understand Jesus Christ as our approach offering. We have examined in detail how the approach offerings of the Old Testament foreshadow Christ laying down his life in the Gospels. We now are looking at many New Testament references—all to one purpose—that we may acquire that right way of believing concerning our Lord Jesus Christ as our approach offering. So, in turn, we may effectually utilize the access and the boldness Christ has achieved for us.

When God's Word says we "have boldness" in Ephesians 3:12 and I John 5:14 or "having. . . boldness" in Hebrews 10:19, it expresses a reality God has wrought for us by the work of Christ. Now it behooves us to manifest this special and distinct *parrhēsia*. This boldness is ours. We <u>have</u> it. But now we must step forth in full assurance, carrying it out.

Perhaps the most remarkable point here is that the achievements of Christ's sacrifice were so extensive that they included the manner of approach as well as the approach itself. The access to God that Christ wrought for us was so complete that the mode of entrée was also accomplished by him. Examining our boldness in Christ provides a glimpse at another one of the multifaceted dimensions of our redemption. As we explore these details of God's Word, the utter completeness of our salvation in Christ staggers the mind.

> Psalm 62:8:
> Trust in him at all times; ye people, pour out your heart before him: God *is* a refuge for us. Selah.

It has always been God's desire for His people to pour out their hearts before Him. We do not enter into God's presence groveling with the head lowered. We enter in with boldness, with a fearless mind. This is how wide the way is opened. We are to have no fear speaking to God. Our hearts should be open unto Him.

> Hebrews 4:16:
> Let us therefore come boldly [*parrhēsia*] unto the throne of grace, that we may obtain mercy, and find grace to help in time of need.

We have boldness that has been accomplished for us in Christ. We can be open with God and confidently pour our hearts out to Him. Christ has wrought a complete and full access for us. We should now renew our minds to the point where we live this spiritual reality.

Hebrews 4:16 says that we come to the throne of grace to find grace, which is divine favor. The sinful human mind has constant difficulty comprehending the grace of God towards us. Grace is undeserved favor and kindness from God. Our approach to God has to be by His undeserved kindness and grace since we are so incapable of acquiring it on our own.

Let us take a moment to consider the superb fellowship Adam enjoyed with God in the Garden of Eden in Genesis. God, who is Spirit, (John 4:24) made Adam in His image (Genesis 1:27). Therefore, God placed His spirit upon Adam so they could freely communicate. Adam partnered with God in working in the Garden. The earth was under Adam's dominion (Genesis 1:28-31). Adam enjoyed an open and productive relationship with God as "second-in-command."

It was not until after Adam's calamitous sin that he feared God and hid from His presence (Genesis 3:8). Man has been cowering in fear since Adam's fall. Consequently, God sent His Son to regain for us this approach and boldness. What grace! The human mind tends to bristle at receiving God's grace. But we had no capacity within ourselves to re-acquire the free and bold approach Adam had lost.

Fallen Man's Approach

Since the fall of Adam and Eve in the Garden, it is human nature to fear when approaching God. After Adam and Eve sinned, their first response is depicted in Genesis 3:8, ". . . and Adam and his wife hid themselves from the presence [face] of Lord God amongst the trees of the garden." Later in verse ten, Adam tells God exactly why he did this: ". . .I was afraid. . ." Before Adam and Eve sinned they did not hide themselves nor were they afraid. They had free access to their Creator. Prior to the fall they had walked face-to-face with God, now they shrank back, retreating from God in fear.

This phrase in Genesis 3:8 is more than a one-time event. It points to an abiding predisposition in the heart of each person from that day forward: to cower, to run from the face of a loving God. Following our human ancestor's catastrophic fall into sin, the proclivity of sinful humans is to run for cover out of fear. This is the opposite of an approach to God with boldness.

What Adam lost on that dismal day in the Garden was the spirit of God within him. He had been created in the image of God. That day, when he sinned, he lost his connection with God. When that "image of God" was lost, the free and direct access he had to God was lost as well. Since that time, at the inner core of man's consciousness is a sense of insecurity in approaching God. This profoundly impacts all of us to this day. Our natural tendency is *not* to approach God with boldness. The very *mental DNA* of fallen humanity has a tendency to shrink back from God. Hence it takes some mental adjustment—or as the Church epistles put it, renewing of the mind—to learn to approach with boldness.

A descriptive example of how fallen man approaches his gods is given in Acts by Paul as he addresses the Athenians.

> Acts 17:22 and 23:
> Then Paul stood in the midst of Mars hill, and said, *Ye men of Athens, I perceive that in all things ye are too superstitious* [*deisidaimon*].
> For as I passed by, and beheld your devotions [*sabasma*], I found an altar with this inscription, To THE UNKNOWN GOD. Whom therefore ye ignorantly worship, him declare I unto you.

Valuable truth in these verses comes from grasping the precise meanings of these Greek words, *deisidaimon* and *sabasma*. These words illustrate the miserable attempt of fallen man to approach and worship God or gods. The Greek word, *deisidaimon*, translated as "too superstitious," literally means, "dread of deities."[6] *Deisidaimon* is made up of two words—*deisi* and *daimon*. *Deisi* means cowering, dread, or fear. A form of this word is used in II Timothy 1:7—*deilias*—referring to a spirit of fear or cowardice. The second word, *daimon*, is commonly translated "devils" in Scripture. Here Paul graphically depicts the worship of fallen man—in dread, cowering before devils.

Concerning the word translated as "devotions" in verse 22, E. W. Bullinger defines the verb form of the word *sabasma*: "to be shy or timid, to shame one's self, to be abased; hence to cherish or pay devotion."[7] The root meaning is "to shrink back from."[8]   This word gets to the root of man's attitude in approaching God after the fall. Humankind shrinks back from God and does not walk with Him face-to-face. These Greek words succinctly describe the worship and approach to God or gods with the fallen nature of humanity—timid, shy, cowering in dread of devils. The Gentile nations struggled to approach their gods with apprehension, a lurking dread. These are the depths to which humanity has descended.[9]   What a sharp contrast to the bold entrance to God that Christ has accomplished for us!

While Acts gives an example of the Gentiles' dread in approaching God, the Israelites had a similar problem. They also had extreme fear in drawing near to God.

> Hebrews 12:18-21:
> For ye are not come [approaching] unto the mount that might be touched, and that burned with fire, nor unto blackness, and darkness, and tempest,
> And the sound of a trumpet, and the voice of words; which *voice* they that heard intreated that the word should not be spoken to them any more:
> (For they could not endure that which was commanded, And if so much as a beast touch the mountain, it shall be stoned, or thrust through with a dart:
> And so terrible was the sight, *that* Moses said, I exceedingly fear and quake:)

These verses sum up the awesome and frightful events of Exodus 19 and 20 in the giving of the Law at Mt. Sinai. The children of Israel begged Moses, "Speak thou with us, and we will hear: but let not God speak with us, lest we die" (Exodus 20:19). Even Moses was afraid (Hebrews 12:21). In contrast to the Gentiles, the Israelites' fear of approaching God was not based on superstition, ignorance or fear of the unknown—but on actual experience! Therefore, we can conclude that natural man's fear and hesitancy to approach God are not entirely misplaced.

Our Approach to God by the Spirit

Christ has restored boldness for us so we should never approach God with shame and dread. By the payment of Christ on the cross, he has restored the free and bold access Adam once had in the garden. Through Christ we can walk face-to-face with our Heavenly Father without shrinking back in fear and self-loathing.

> Romans 8:15-18:
> For ye have not received the spirit of bondage again to fear; but ye have received the Spirit of adoption [sonship], whereby we cry, Abba, Father.
> The Spirit itself beareth witness with our spirit, that we are the children of God:
> And if [since] children, then heirs; heirs of God, and joint-heirs with Christ; if [since] so be that we suffer with *him*, that we may be also glorified together.
> For I reckon that the sufferings of this present time *are* not worthy *to be compared* with the glory which shall be revealed in us.

Verse 15: "For ye have not received the spirit of bondage again to fear. . ." once more expresses the approach to God of fallen humanity. The whole scope of humanity's character and lifestyle was pervaded by serving their gods in fear and bondage. The Gentile nations, instead of reverencing the Creator, cowered in fear before devils. God's chosen people, Israel, also cringed in bondage at times.

The last phrase of verse 15 is one of the most poignant statements in the Bible— ". . .but ye have received the Spirit of adoption [sonship, *huiothesia*], whereby we cry, Abba, Father." Abba is an Aramaic word meaning "father or daddy," suggesting a near and dear relationship. The utter pathos of these words touches the human heart. Being made sons—*hious*, adult sons with full rights and privileges—we entreat our Father in the most intimate terms, as a tender small child, "Abba, Father." This phrase richly combines our legal position as *hious* of God with the tender-hearted and precious access we have to our loving Father. We, as sons of God, come to Him as dear children on the most intimate terms, calling Him "Abba" or "Daddy." God is not glowering at us in exasperation. We can speak to God freely with our hearts open.

Verse 15 also states that this wonderful approach to God is by the spirit of sonship. This sonship spirit, or *"pneuma huiothesia"* in Greek, facilitates our access to God. Of course, this sonship spirit is the same as the gift of holy spirit God has given us in the new birth. Sonship is one of the attributes of this holy spirit inside us. We have received the sonship spirit, "whereby [by which] we cry, Abba, Father."[10] By the holy spirit within that we exclaim, "Abba, Father!" By the spirit we have this intimate and open access.

Verse 16 continues with this topic of approach by the spirit: "The Spirit itself [the gift of holy spirit] beareth witness with our spirit [innermost part of our being], that we are the children of God." How exactly does the spirit "bear witness?" Some have said this witness of the spirit here in Romans 8:16 is the fruit of the spirit.[11] I would suggest the nine manifestations of the spirit listed in I Corinthians 12:8-10 would better qualify as the witness of the spirit.

Romans 8:15 says by the holy spirit of sonship, "we cry Abba, Father." This word "cry" suggests utterance. Later Romans 8:26 states: "...the spirit itself maketh intercession with groanings which cannot be uttered." Again, this suggests some form of spoken words. In Acts 2:4 at the inauguration of the Church, God's Word declares, "And they were all filled with the Holy Ghost, and began to speak with other tongues, as the Spirit gave them utterance." Here on the Day of Pentecost, the Holy Spirit is giving them utterance. What are they doing? Speaking in tongues! This utterance was a witness or a sign that they had received the gift of holy spirit from God.

Later on in Acts 10, the household of Cornelius spoke in tongues (verse 46). This manifestation was taken as proof that these Gentiles, "...have received the holy spirit as well as we..." Throughout the Book of Acts, speaking in tongues is a witness of having received the holy spirit.

Jesus foretold of this sign:

> Mark 16:17:
> And these signs shall follow them that believe; In my name shall they cast out devils; they shall speak with new tongues;

Jesus called speaking in tongues a sign. I Corinthians 14:22 also says speaking in tongues is for a sign.

Romans 8:16 says, "The Spirit itself beareth witness with our spirit, that we are the children of God." This means that the holy spirit, in operation in our lives, affirms to our innermost heart that we are indeed sons of God. The utterance manifestation of speaking in tongues bears witness and gives assurance that the spirit within is a reality. As we will see, this assurance that the holy spirit in operation gives us, is one of those indispensable qualities needed to approach God with boldness.

Our *Parrhēsia* by the Spirit in I John

The word *parrhēsia*, meaning boldness, is used four times in I John. In the context of this word are many practical keys to applying this extraordinary *parrhēsia* we have in Christ. It is remarkable that in the context of each usage the manifesting or the evidence of the spirit is mentioned.

1. I John 2:28 speaks of *parrhēsia* at his Coming. Just previously, verse 27 refers to manifesting the spirit.

> I John 2:27 and 28:
> But the anointing [of holy spirit] which ye have received of him abideth in you, and ye need not that any man teach you: but as the same anointing [of holy spirit] teacheth you of all things, and is truth, and is no lie, and even as it hath taught you, ye shall **abide in him**.
> And now, little children, **abide in him**; that, when he shall appear, we may have confidence [*parrhēsia*], and not be ashamed before him at his coming.

Verse 27 refers to the anointing of holy spirit teaching us. When the holy spirit is manifested by teaching us, we "shall abide in him." Then, as we abide in him, when he appears we may have *parrhēsia* at his Coming.

2. I John 3:21 refers to having *parrhēsia* towards God. Verse 24 it says, "And hereby we know that he abideth in us by the Spirit which he hath given us." One scholar says of this usage: "A further distinctive aspect of *parrhēsia* may be seen, however, in verse 24. It is given with the

presence of the *pneuma* in us. . . **parrhēsia to God is to be found where God indwells by the Spirit. . .**"¹² This, indeed, is the point: our *parrhēsia* is by the gift of holy spirit within us.

3. I John 4:17 again says we have boldness.

> I John 4:13-18:
> Hereby know we that we dwell in him, and he in us, because he hath given us of his Spirit.
> And we have seen and do testify that the Father sent the Son *to be* the Saviour of the world.
> Whosoever shall confess that Jesus is the Son of God, God dwelleth in him, and he in God.
> And we have known and believed the love that God hath to us. God is love; and he that dwelleth in love dwelleth in God, and God in him.
> Herein is our love made perfect, that we may have **boldness [*parrhēsia*]** in the day of judgment: because as he is, so are we in this world.
> There is no fear in love; but perfect love casteth out fear: because fear hath torment. He that feareth is not made perfect in love.

In the immediate context, verse 13 states: "Hereby know we that we dwell in him, and he in us, because he hath given us of his Spirit." By manifesting the spirit we have the witness. This leads directly to our love being made perfect and our *parrhēsia* in verse 17.

4. I John 5:14 is the final use of *parrhēsia* in I John.

> I John 5:14 and 15:
> And this is **the** confidence [*parrhēsia*] that we have in him, that, if we ask any thing according to his will, he heareth us:

And if we know that he hear us, whatsoever we ask, we know that we have the petitions that we desired of him.

Previously, verses 6-12 are about the witness of the spirit within the believer. Our *parrhēsia* we have in him, and the certainty we have in prayer, rests upon manifesting the witness of the spirit as mentioned in the preceding context.

Each of the four uses of *parrhēsia* in I John relates to the operation of the gift of God's holy spirit within us. This fits with what we have considered in a previous chapter from Ephesians 2:18: "…we both have access by one Spirit unto the Father." Approaching God with boldness involves utilizing the holy spirit God has given us.

Utilizing Our Boldness: Approaching with Full Assurance

Hebrews 10:22 tell us how to utilize the boldness spoken of in Hebrews 10:19.

> Hebrews 10:22:
> Let us draw near with a true heart in full assurance [*plērophoria*] of faith, having our hearts sprinkled from an evil conscience, and our bodies washed with pure water.

Here we are exhorted to "draw near." This is what we are to do: approach God in prayer. Then the remainder of this verse tells us precisely *how* we are to do it: **"with a true heart in full assurance of faith. . ."** This is the very essence of the matter. Here we have the *keys to the castle*. This is how we get into the throne room: we are to approach God in full assurance of believing.

Christians often confuse God's job with their job. They mix up what God has done with what they are instructed to do. So many of the New Testament texts we have examined are rich with what God has done through Christ. But Hebrews 10:22 gives specifics as to what we are to do. We should carefully examine these words and diligently carry them out.

"Full assurance" is the Greek word *plērophoria*, meaning full persuasion with **absolute certainty, without doubt or hesitation**.[13] *Plērophoria* is also defined as "unshakable conviction."[14] When it comes to approaching our Heavenly Father, we should not get bogged down with pious and confused ambiguities. We are to come before God with candid confidence and full certainty, holding nothing back.

In Hebrews 10:22, "full assurance of faith," is *plērophoria pisteōs* in Greek. *Pisteōs*, translated "of faith" is genitive of origin. Faith is the cause or the origin of the "full persuasion." Your certainty in approaching God without doubt or hesitation proceeds out of your faith. Perhaps *The Amplified Bible* puts it most beautifully: ". . .in unqualified assurance and absolute conviction engendered by faith."[15] The genesis of our unqualified conviction is our believing in what God has promised in His Word.

The verb form of *plērophoria* is used in Romans 4:20 and 21 speaking of Abraham:

> Romans 4:20 and 21:
> He staggered not at the promise of God through unbelief; but was strong in faith, giving glory to God;
> And being fully persuaded [*plērophoreō*] that, what he [God] had promised, he [God] was able also to perform.

Just as Abraham staggered not at God's promises, we should not waver at God's promises to us. As Abraham was strong in believing, so should we be empowered in our believing of God's Word. Abraham gave glory to God. Likewise, we should magnify God and His ability, not our own. Abraham got to the point of being fully persuaded—he believed God's words. We too should become totally convinced that God's ability and God's promise are in agreement. We should have full certainty that God makes good on His promises. Then we will see God perform His Word in our lives.

> Hebrews 11:6:
> But without faith *it is* impossible to please *him*: for he that cometh to [approaches] God must believe that he is, and *that* he is a rewarder of them that diligently seek him.

It could hardly be stated any more bluntly: without faith it is impossible to please God. This is not set forth as an optional suggestion. To approach God you *must* believe two things: one, that God is, that He is there; and, two, you *must* believe that He is a rewarder of them that diligently seek Him. This second point involves approaching with persistance. What is most significant here is that we *must* believe that diligent seeking gets results. We *must* believe that God rewards those who are persistent to seek and to approach Him. Once we are fully persuaded that God rewards the diligent seeker *then* we will continually persist in bold approach. The second great key in approaching God is persistance.

Just previous to Hebrews 11:6 this issue of rewards for persistance is addressed:

> Hebrews 10:35 and 36:
> Cast not away therefore your confidence [*parrhēsia*], which hath great recompence of reward.
> For ye have need of patience, that, after ye have done the will of God, ye might receive the promise.

Because it has great reward, it would be a shame to cast away our *parrhēsia*. Yet this is one of the pitfalls that we may face concerning this wonderful boldness we have in Christ: we may, of our own free will, cast it away and give up. When God's people suffer disappointments and difficulties, they are often tempted to quit praying and to stop using the access and the boldness they have in Christ Jesus. Some of these believers addressed in Hebrews had lost their material possessions, been ridiculed and subjected to legal prosecution for their believing in Christ (Hebrews 10:32-34). At this point of extreme difficulty, they were tempted to be discouraged and say, "what's the use—why bother praying?" At this juncture, God's exhortation is: "cast not away your boldness, which has great recompense of reward. For ye have need of patience..."

One of the outstanding paragons of approaching God in prayer in the New Testament is Epaphras. He is mentioned in Colossians 1:7, 4:12 and Philemon 23. In Colossians 1:7 Epaphras is called a "faithful [*pistos*] minister of Christ." Then Colossians 4:12 and 13 tells of the characteristics of this faithful minister.

> Colossians 4:12 and 13:
> Epaphras, who is *one* of you, a servant of Christ, saluteth you, always labouring fervently for you in prayers, that ye may stand perfect and complete [*plērophoria*, fully persuaded] in all the will of God.

> For I bear him record, that he hath a great zeal for you, and them *that are* in Laodicea, and them in Hierapolis.

Little is known of this notable Christian leader. But what is briefly stated here speaks volumes to those of us who aspire to be faithful servants of Christ. What did this faithful man do? He always labored fervently for the believers in prayer. He faithfully persevered in approaching God for His people. He did not "cast away" his *parrhēsia*. He obviously believed that diligent seeking paid off. He was a living example of the Biblical exhortation to "pray without ceasing."[16]

Epaphras was not only faithful but, as verse 13 states, he had the zeal and the drive to persist. Herein is another notable attribute of a faithful minister—the blend of both passion and unwavering consistence.

We see God's will for His people reflected in the prayers of Epaphras. The last phrase of verse 12 in the *New Revised Standard Version* reads, ". . .that you may stand mature and fully assured in everything that God wills." God desires us to be fully assured in all the will of God. Once we get to the point of full persuasion, like Abraham, we will know that God makes good on His promises. We will not vacillate with anxiety but be as Epaphras prayed, "fully persuaded in all the will of God."

How do we reach this point of full persuasion? There are two ways: by ingesting the Word of God, and operating the spirit of God. Romans 10:17 states: "So then faith *cometh* by hearing, and hearing by the word of God." As we feed on God's Word, it engenders faith. Colossians 3:16 says, "Let the word of Christ dwell in you richly in all wisdom…" As the word about what Christ has accomplished takes up residence in our minds, believing will emerge. Jeremiah said, "Thy words were found, and I did eat them; and thy word was unto me the joy and rejoicing of mine heart..."(Jeremiah 15:16).

> I Thessalonians 1:5:
> For our gospel came not unto you in word only, but also in power, and in the Holy Ghost, and in much assurance [*plērophoria*]; as ye know what manner of men we were among you for your sake.

The words of God's Word should come unto us "not in word only" but in power and in the holy spirit and in full assurance. The holy spirit was in manifestation, operated with power. This is how you reach that full persuasion.[17] The *Twentieth Century Translation* says that the Word of God came with power and "...much certainty due to holy spirit."

This verse so characterized my life. I grappled with doubt and uncertainty about my believing in God until I began to see the power of the holy spirit in my life. When I manifested the power of God in my life, then those doubts I had about God and His Word withered and died.

At the young age of 18, I learned that each manifestation of the holy spirit was not a gift endowed on a special few but was rather received by believing. Weakness in my Christian life was replaced by deep conviction when I saw the operation of the manifestation of the spirit in my own life. However, I never received the holy spirit into demonstration in my life until I understood that I received, not by my own pious goodness, but by pure full-hearted believing.

Our aim should be to reach full persuasion concerning our access to God. Filling our minds and hearts to the brim with the glorious realities of the Scripture will enable us to attain the state of "full assurance of faith."

> I John 5:14 and 15:
> And this is **the** confidence [*parrhēsia*] that we have in him, that, if we ask any thing according to his will, he heareth us:
> And if we know that he hear us, whatsoever we ask, we know that we have the petitions that we desired of him.

Verse 14 defines **the** "special and distinct" boldness we have and how to carry it out. This boldness is of such an extraordinary nature that ". . .if we ask any thing according to His will, He heareth us." What goodness and grace God has toward us!

Verse 15 speaks to the topic of reaching the point of total certainty in believing. "And if we **know** that he hears us, whatsoever we ask, we **know** that we have the petitions that we desired of him." Once the will of God is ascertained in a situation and you go to God with your request, you know—not question or doubt—that God hears you. Verse 15 says we are to "know"—not waffle, not hesitate, not doubt. This is the key: to approach God speaking freely with full certainty that He hears and answers your prayer. Bowing and scraping before God, with a sense of desperate foreboding, do not bring results. In approaching God, whatsoever you shall ask in prayer, **believing**, you shall receive (Matthew 21:22). Your bold approach is not by your own goodness but by the work of our Lord Jesus Christ and your consequent believing in that work.

I John 3:19-22:
> And hereby we know that we are of the truth, and shall assure [persuade] our hearts before him.
>
> For if our heart condemn us, God is greater than our heart, and knoweth all things.
>
> Beloved, if our heart condemn us not, *then* have we confidence [*parrhēsia*] toward God.
>
> And whatsoever we ask, we receive of him, because we keep his commandments, and do those things that are pleasing in his sight.

Verse 19 speaks of "assuring our hearts before him." The word "assure" can be translated as "persuade." Again, we are to be persuaded—not in a state of double-mindedness or uncertainty. Believing assurance before God is what brings unfailing answers to prayer.

What a joyful challenge it is to rise up and walk in all the richness and glory of our redemption. In operating this remarkable boldness we have, we can make life here on earth a thrilling journey. As we walk hand in hand with our Heavenly Father, we know that He hears and answers our prayers.

Notes

1. Kenneth Wuest, *Wuest's Word Studies from the Greek New Testament*, Volume II, 73.

2. E. W. Bullinger, *Lexicon*, 354.

3. In English "a" (or "an") is called an indefinite article while the definite article is "the." In Greek when the definite article is placed before an abstract noun, it is used to "point out individual identity" and gives "a determined concrete application" making the word "special and distinct." See H. E. Dana and Julius Mantey, *A Manual Grammar of the Greek New Testament* (New York: The MacMillan Company, 1955), 137.

Curtis Vanghan and Virtus E. Gideon, *A Greek Grammar of the New Testament* (Nashville, TN: Broadman, 1979), 81. Referring to the Greek definite article: "The student must therefore pay most careful attention to its use, he must not think that it is used arbitrarily or without reason [as in English], because he finds it difficult to express its force in English." The distinctive force of the Greek article is to draw attention to a word or an idea. In the Greek, the definite article points out the special and distinctness of the noun.

Robertson, 756: "It is generally used as a pointer. And is indeed its most basic use."

4. Chris Geer first brought this usage of the Greek definite article to my attention. He expresses *pistis/pisteuo*, when associated with the definite article, as "the right way of believing," (Gartmore Weekly Tape 115). Audiocassette.

Also see: Chris Geer, "THE [Right Way of] Believing," *Future Considerations*, Issue 23 (March 1991): 1-8.

5. Robertson says "of him" in Ephesians 3:12 is "objective genitive" meaning the faith **concerning** him. See Archibald Robertson, *Word Pictures in the New Testament*, (Nashville, TN: Broadman, 1931), Vol. IV, 532.

6. In Shakespeare's *Othello,* the name of a pious woman who is murdered is "Desdemona." Her name is taken from this Greek word.

7. Bullinger, *Lexicon,* 903 s.v. *sabasma.*

8. *Kittels*, Volume 7, 1669. Ceslas Spicq defines the word *sabasma* as, "very attentive to omens and dreams, careful to avoid defilement, carrying out multiple purifications, reciting prayers suited for the given circumstances, worshipping of images." Ceslas Spicq, *Theological Lexicon of the New Testament*, translated and edited by James Ernest (1978, Peabody, Mass: Hendrickson, 1994), Volume I, 306.

9. Perhaps Romans 1:18-32 best describes the morass into which humanity has plunged.

10. New American Standard Bible says, ". . .by which we cry. . ."

11. Albert Barnes *New Testament Commentary* says of the witness of Romans 8:16, " It is his to renew the heart; to sanctify the soul; to produce 'love, joy, peace, long-suffering, gentleness, goodness, faith, meekness, temperance,' Galatians 5:22,23. If a man has these, he has evidence of the witnessing of the Spirit with his spirit."

12. Kittels, Volume V, page 881.

13. Spicq, Volume III, p. 120.

14. Kittels, Volume VI, page 310.

15. The accuracy of the *Amplified Bible* here is eye opening. It renders "of faith" in the genitive of origin (in the Greek text) as "engendered by faith." In English both "engender" and "genitive" come from the same root word.

16. I Thessalonians 5:17.

17. Robertson, Volume IV, page 11: ". . .the full confidence that comes with the holy spirit. . ."

7

Without Blemish before Him in Love

Ephesians 3:12:
In whom [Christ] we have boldness and access with confidence by the faith of him.

Jesus Christ, as our approach offering to God, was so complete and so effective that it staggers the human mind. The heart can hardly take in the full and bold access to God Christ has achieved for us by his suffering and death at Calvary. In spite of our systemic human insecurity in approaching God, phrases like this shine from the Word of God: "in whom we have boldness and access with confidence..."

Our access to God is by the offering of Jesus Christ. Through Christ's sacrifice on our behalf, we have been reconciled to God. Unlike the multiple and repeated approach offerings of the Old Testament, Christ suffered and died only once, that—as I Peter 3:18 states—"he might bring us to God."

The word "access" of Ephesians 3:12 means an "escorted introduction." Once we have been escorted into the presence of God, how does God see us? What is His assessment of us? As we stand in His sight, how does He evaluate us?

> Ephesians 1:4:
> According as he hath chosen us in him before the foundation of the world, that we should be holy and without blame [without blemish, *amōmos*] before him in love:

"Holy and without blemish"—this is God's assessment of us. In His judgment and in His opinion, we are holy and without blemish. ". . .That we should be," is more accurate when rendered in the infinitive, "to be." The *New American Bible* says, "as he chose us in him, before the foundation of the world, **to be** holy and without blemish before him."[1] This verse is speaking of our complete and perfect standing before God that we have in Christ. It is not stating what "should be" but what has already been done by Christ.

> Colossians 1:22:
> In the body of his flesh through death, to present you holy and unblameable [without blemish, *amōmos*] and unreproveable in his sight.

In God's sight, our standing before the presence of God is "without blemish" as voiced by both Ephesians and Colossians. God's evaluation of us as sons of God is "holy and without blemish."

The first clause of Colossians 1:22 tells us how we received this unblemished status, "In the body of his flesh through death . . ." Previously, we learned that our approach to God was accomplished by the work of Christ. Similarly, our standing before God after we have approached, is also by Christ's sacrifice. Our holiness, our *blemish-free status*, is by our Lord's death on the cross, not by our own good works. We should not work to become what has already been achieved. This is often the lamentable plight of Christians today who labor to complete what God has already brought into full fruition in Christ Jesus.

> Philippians 2:15:
> That ye may be [become] blameless and harmless, the sons of God, without rebuke [without blemish, *amōmos*], in the midst of a crooked and perverse nation, among whom ye shine as lights in the world;

The *New International Version* renders the first phase of this verse, "so that you may **become** blameless and pure..." This—in contrast to Ephesians 1:4—is what we are to achieve in our walks: God wants us to *become*, by the freedom of our will, "blameless and harmless." However, in the *King James Version* the next phrase, "the sons of God, without blemish," is what we already have through what Christ has accomplished for us on the cross. The *Amplified Bible* reads, "That you may show yourselves to be blameless *and* guileless, innocent *and* uncontaminated, children of God without blemish. . ." Since we are children of God without blemish, we should apply ourselves to become faultless and uncontaminated in this evil world.

Please allow me to reiterate. You are without blemish in God's sight. Due to inexact Biblical translation this may be new for you; but this is God's opinion of you. This may not be the opinion you hold of yourself. Have you ever thought of yourself as "without blemish?" This is yet another one of those wonderful new birth realities we have as sons of God: God sees us without flaw and without blemish.

Without Blemish in Leviticus

We will now look at Leviticus, in the Old Testament, to see that God required both sacrifices and priests to be without blemish if they were to approach Him. Also, keep in mind that both the sacrifice and the priest of the Old Testament foreshadowed the coming Messiah. Just as the Christ they anticipated, the sacrifices and the priesthood were to be without blemish.

The central issue of the Book of Leviticus concerns approaching God. According to the revelation of Leviticus, no sacrifice or priest could approach God unless it was without blemish and without spot. As noted below, the Hebrew word *qarab*, meaning to approach or bring near, is often used in these passages.

> Leviticus 1:3:
> If his offering *be* a burnt sacrifice of the herd, let him offer [*qarab*] a male without blemish. . .
>
> Leviticus 22:17-25:
> And the Lord spake unto Moses, saying,
> Speak unto Aaron, and to his sons, and unto all the children of Israel, and say unto them, Whatsoever *he be* of the house of Israel, or of the strangers in Israel, that will offer [*qarab*] his oblation [*qorban*, approach offering] for all his vows, and for all his freewill offerings, which they will offer [*qarab*] unto the Lord for a burnt offering;
> *Ye shall offer* at your own will a male without blemish, of the beeves [bulls], of the sheep, or of the goats.
> *But* whatsoever hath a blemish, *that* shall ye not offer [*qarab*]: for it shall not be acceptable for you.
> [Verse 21] And whosoever offereth [*qarab*] a sacrifice of peace offerings unto the LORD to accomplish *his*

vow, or a freewill offering in beeves or sheep, it shall be perfect to be accepted; there shall be no blemish therein.

Blind, or broken, or maimed, or having a wen [festering or running sore, *NIV*], or scurvy, or scabbed, ye shall not offer [*qarab*] these unto the LORD, nor make an offering by fire of them upon the altar unto the LORD.

Either a bullock or a lamb that hath any thing superfluous [deformed] or lacking in his parts [stunted], that mayest thou offer *for* a freewill offering; but for a vow it shall not be accepted.

Ye shall not offer [*qarab*] unto the LORD that which is bruised, or crushed, or broken, or cut; neither shall ye make *any offering thereof* in your land.

Neither from a stranger's hand shall ye offer [*qarab*] the bread of your God of any of these; because their corruption *is* in them, *and* blemishes *be* in them: they shall not be accepted for you.

This revelation defines precisely what a blemished sacrifice was. No sacrifices could be presented to God that were defective or flawed. Any blemish or fault made the sacrifice unacceptable to God. There was no approach to God with any defective or deformed offerings. They were to be "perfect to be accepted" (verse 21).

God has not lowered His standards to accommodate us! Whether Old or New Covenant, God requires those that approach Him to be without blemish. This is why He has created us in Christ, sons of God, without blemish. Now we can approach God as living sacrifices because we are flawless in His sight.

The priests who approached God in service were also to be without blemish or imperfection.

Leviticus 21:16-23:
And the Lord spake unto Moses, saying,
Speak unto Aaron, saying, Whosoever *he be* of thy seed in their generations that hath *any* blemish, let him not approach [*qarab*] to offer [*qarab*] the bread of his God.
For whatsoever man *he be* that hath a blemish, he shall not approach [*qarab*]: a blind man, or a lame, or he that hath a flat nose, or any thing superfluous [deformed],
Or a man that is brokenfooted, or brokenhanded,
Or crookbackt, or a dwarf, or that hath a blemish in his eye, or be scurvy, or scabbed, or hath his stones broken;
No man that hath a blemish of the seed of Aaron the priest shall come nigh to offer [*qarab*] the offerings of the LORD made by fire: he hath a blemish; he shall not come nigh to offer [*qarab*] the bread of his God.
He shall eat the bread of his God, *both* of the most holy, and of the holy.
Only he shall not go in unto the vail, nor come nigh unto the altar, because he hath a blemish; that he profane not my sanctuaries: for I the LORD do sanctify [make holy] them.

Under the Old Covenant, only those of the line of Aaron could approach God to serve in the tabernacle. However, not only did one have to be of the right lineage, one had to be physically faultless in order to approach. Without these qualifications one would defile the tabernacle.

We are qualified to approach God because Christ has made us qualified. We can approach God boldly with a fearless mind. Because, as sons of God in the new birth, we are of the right lineage and faultless in God's sight.

Our Cleansing in Jesus Christ

As God's sacrifice on our behalf, Jesus Christ was without blemish and without spot.

> I Peter 1:18 and 19:
> Forasmuch as ye know that ye were not redeemed with corruptible things, *as* silver and gold, from your vain conversation *received* by tradition from your fathers;
> But with the precious blood of Christ, as of a lamb **without blemish [*amōmos*] and without spot**:

> Hebrews 9:14:
> How much more shall the blood of Christ, who through the eternal Spirit offered himself **without spot** [without blemish, *amōmos*] to God, purge your conscience from dead works to serve the living God?

Since Christ as the Lamb of God was without blemish and without spot, so are we—legally without blemish in the sight of God. This is possible because of our *identification* with Christ. In a legal sense, God sees us as identical to Christ. Galatians 2:20 refers to this identification with Christ: " I am crucified with Christ. . ." Also, Romans 6:6 expresses the same truth by stating that our old man nature was crucified with Christ. When Christ died, all our sin died with him. All our blemishes, all our shortcomings, faults and failings died with Christ. That is why we stand before God faultless. We are without blemish because we share fully with Christ in his death.

Much of the Church Epistles echo this concept of our identification with Christ. Some of us have glimpsed this great truth doctrinally; yet in practice, ". . .the heart is slow to learn, what the mind beholds at every turn." [2]

II Corinthians 5:21:
For he hath made him *to be* sin [offering] for us, who knew no sin; that we might be made the righteousness of God in him.

For accuracy, the word "offering" should be supplied after "sin." Jesus Christ was our sin offering. Just like the sin offering of the Old Testament, Jesus bore all our sins. All of our sin has been transferred to an innocent substitute, who was without spot or blemish. In the death of this substitute, all of the claims of a just and perfect God have been satisfied. In turn, God's righteousness has been transferred to us.

We are righteous now. Now we are holy and without blemish before God's sight. All our sin, all our inadequacy to stand before a just and perfect God has been borne away by Jesus Christ. As our sin offering, he carried all our iniquity up to Calvary.

While a crucial point of the sin offering was that it carried away sin, there was an even more significant aspect. The overarching focus of the sin offering was its cleansing power.[3] The blood of that sin offering cleansed and purified. Hebrews 9:13 and 14 accentuates this truth:

> For if the blood of bulls and of goats, and the ashes of an heifer sprinkling the unclean, sanctifieth to the purifying of the flesh:
> How much more shall the blood of Christ, who through the eternal Spirit offered himself without spot to God, purge [*katharizō*, purify] your conscience from dead works to serve the living God?

The Greek word *katharizō*, means to cleanse and purify without any stain or impurity. In the secular Greek, *katharizō* is also used in the sense of spotless and without blemish.[4]

The blood of the sin offering ceremonially purified those under the Old Covenant. The offering of Christ's blood does so much more for us! His blood purified our "conscience from dead works to serve the living God."

The greatness of the sin offering of Jesus Christ was in its cleansing power. We stand in the presence of God with no uncleanness. In a legal sense, we are righteous, judicially cleared, declared innocent. We are without sin, without stain, without blemish before God. "Dead works" do not have the power to cleanse the conscience and remove the guilt of sin, but the blood of Christ does.

> Hebrews 10:19 and 22:
> Having therefore, brethren, boldness to enter into the holiest by the blood of Jesus. . .
>
> . . .Let us draw near with a true heart in full assurance of faith, having our hearts sprinkled from an evil conscience, and our bodies washed with pure water.

As we consider these verses that are filled with Old Testament imagery, we need to recall that there was only one time under the Mosaic system that anyone ever approached God in the most holy place. Only on the Day of Atonement, once a year, did the high priest enter into the holy of holies. When verses 19 and 20 speak of entering in through the veil there is only one parallel event in the Old Testament—the Day of Atonement.

On that Day of Atonement as the high priest entered, his body was washed with water (Leviticus 16:4b) and the blood of the sin offering was sprinkled (Leviticus 16:11

and 14). When Hebrews 10:22 states we are to draw near, "... having our hearts sprinkled from an evil conscience, and our bodies washed with pure water," this is a direct reference to the Day of Atonement. Although Hebrews never uses the exact words "Day of Atonement," many times this most important day in the Old Testament is referenced.[5] The paramount theme of Hebrews is entering into God's presence, and it was exclusively on that one day that the entry into the holy of holies occurred.

These phrases in Hebrews 10:22 express New Covenant realities in Old Covenant terminology. Old Testament acts are used to describe what Christ has accomplished for us in the new birth. The two main symbols of cleansing and purification of the Old Covenant were sprinkling with the blood of a sin offering, and the washing of water.[6] Both are mentioned in Hebrews 10:22 to express the utter totality of our purity by the blood of Christ.

In the Old Testament system, there was no approach to God without cleansing. This truth was written in the Law time and time again. The unclean—the impure—could not approach God; this is a universal truth spanning all administrations. Our approach to God rests solely on the purifying effects of the offering of our Lord Jesus Christ.

". . .Our hearts sprinkled from an evil conscience, and our bodies washed with pure water," is what God has done by His holy spirit in us. The heart totally purified is a reference to the "new man, which after God is created in righteousness and true holiness" (Ephesians 4:24b). "Our bodies washed with pure water" is also a vivid expression of what the gift of holy spirit does in the "new man"—the new spirit nature in all of its totality.

The two verbs "sprinkled" and "washed" in Hebrews 10:22, are perfect passive participles in the Greek. The perfect tense refers to "an action that took place in the past, the results of which have continued to the present."[7] We draw near to God with a true heart in full assurance, our hearts **having been** sprinkled and our bodies **having been** washed with pure water. As a perfect participle, this second part of verse 22 describes a "completed action with present effects."[8] This completed action is what God has accomplished in us by Christ's work in the new birth. "Let us draw near with a true heart in full assurance of faith," is what we ought to do. However, our hearts having been sprinkled from an evil conscience, and our bodies having been washed with pure water, is already new birth reality, having been accomplished for us in Christ.

> I Peter 1:2:
> Elect according to the foreknowledge of God the Father, through sanctification of the Spirit, unto obedience and sprinkling of the blood of Jesus Christ: Grace unto you, and peace, be multiplied.

Here, as in Hebrews 10:22, the sprinkling of the blood is used to express what the gift of holy spirit accomplishes within us. God's work in Christ in the inner man is vividly illustrated in sacrificial language.

When Hebrews 10:22 says, ". . .and our bodies washed [*louō*] with pure water" this is again Old Testament imagery. "Our bodies washed with pure water" is not any more literal than being sprinkled with the blood of a sin offering is literal. This phrase, as with the previous one, is using Old Testament imagery to depict the greatness of the new birth.

Titus 3:5 and 6:
Not by works of righteousness which we have done, but according to his mercy he saved us, by the washing [*loutron*] of regeneration, and renewing of the Holy Ghost [spirit];
Which he shed on us abundantly through Jesus Christ our Saviour;

Here Titus augments our understanding of ". . .and our bodies washed with pure water." Our washing is by the holy spirit. Whether reading English or Greek, the same basic word is used in Titus 3:5 and Hebrews 10:22. While Hebrews 10:22 strongly implies that our washing is what the gift of holy spirit has done in us, Titus 3:5 is explicit: we are saved by the washing of holy spirit.[9]

The two primary symbols of cleansing and purification of the Old Covenant were sprinkling with the blood of a sin offering and the washing of water. Both are employed in Hebrews 10:22 to express the completeness of our cleansing in Christ.

The blood of Christ has cleansed our conscience so we can serve not a dead God but a living God! Our God is living. He is moving. He is active in this world today. A vital part of our service to Him is approaching Him in prayer and making our requests known. *We can* come before the presence of God. *We can* approach the loving gaze of our Heavenly Father.

When God looks at us He sees us as pure and faultless, identified with His Son. Regardless of our human failings and sins, God has placed us as sons of God, holy and without blemish, before Him in love.

With such a value placed on our approach and standing before God, the days of our lives should be spent exercising that privilege. As the minutes and hours of our days are taken up with errands and phone calls, let us continually call on Him who has waited so long and done so much that His people could commune with Him.

Notes

1. The NIV and NRSV as well as the NAB renders the infinitive accurately, "to be."

2. Line from poem by Edna St. Vincent Millay.

3. Jacob Milgrom, a preeminent Leviticus scholar, insists that the Old Testament "sin offering" is a mistranslation and should be called a "purification offering." He quotes ancient rabbis who shared his views. Milgrom shows how the word for sin offering in the Hebrew could be rendered purification. He shows how so many of the uses of the sin offering in the Old Testament were for purification alone and had nothing to do with sin. (See Milgrom, *Leviticus 1-16 The Anchor Bible*, 253.) Hebrews 9:13, 14, and especially verse 21 support his view. Jesus Christ as our sin offering is more directly represented by the trespass offering. Isaiah 53:10 calls Christ a trespass offering.

4. Liddell and Scott's, 388.

5. See my article: **The Far View,** "Ascension Day, Foreshadowed by the Day of Atonement; Explained in Hebrews." (May, June 2001).

6. See Hebrews 9:21 and 22a, Leviticus 14:6 and 7, 16:19. From these references it is clear the sprinkling of blood represented cleansing. In regard to cleansing by washing in water see: Leviticus 14:8 and 9. On the Day of Atonement the high priest washed before putting on the holy garments (Leviticus 16:4). In Exodus 29:4 and 17 and 30:18-21 both priests and sacrifices were washed with

water before approaching God. As living sacrifices we have been cleansed by Christ's complete sacrifice.

Also the ashes of a red heifer mixed with water symbolized cleansing. Both symbols of ceremonial cleansing are mentioned in Hebrews 9:13: " . . .the **blood** of bulls and of goats, and the **ashes** of an heifer **sprinkling** the unclean, sanctifieth to the purifying of the flesh." See my article: *The Far View,* "The Red Heifer Sin Offering Parallels Christ." (May 2000).

7. Spiros Zodhiates, *Word Study New Testament* (Chattanooga TN: AMG, 1991), 867.

Machen, says "the perfect tenses denote the present state resultant upon a past action." See J. Gresham Machen, *New Testament Greek for Beginners* (Toronto, Canada: Macmillan, 1923), 187.

8. William D. Mounce, *Greek for the Rest of Us* (Grand Rapids, MI: Zondervan, 2003), 179.

9. For our understanding it is helpful to render the Greek words, *pneuma hagion*, as "holy spirit" rather than "the Holy Ghost" as the *King James Version* does. In the Greek there is no definite article placed before *pneuma* in Titus 3:5. Also, translating the Greek word, *pneuma,* as "Ghost" instead of "spirit" is profoundly unhelpful. Also the gift of the holy spirit that God gives at the new birth should not be capitalized since it is not referring to God, Himself, but to His wonderful gift.

8

Holy before Him in Love

In this study we are considering the phrase in Ephesians 1:4: "holy and without blame before him in love." The breathtaking beauty of this phrase is obscured by inconsistent translation and our lack of understanding. To crack open this phrase and get the glorious truth out of it, we must first clear up the translation. Then we can increase our understanding of how these words are used elsewhere in the Bible.

> Ephesians 1:4:
> According as he hath chosen us in him before the foundation of the world, that we should be holy [*hagios*] and without blame [*amōmos,* without blemish] before him in love:

In the last chapter, we corrected the inadequate translation of the Greek word, *amōmos*. *Amōmos* should be rendered "without blemish." Once this was cleared up, we then looked at passages in Leviticus which defined "without blemish" in Old Covenant terms. Most importantly, we saw **why** one should be without blemish. The whole point and purpose of being without blemish was to approach God. In order to approach God by way of the tabernacle as a priest or sacrifice, one had to be without blemish. In examining the New Testament, we observed that God had not downgraded His standards to accommodate our pathetic state. But rather, by the complete work of Christ as a perfect sacrifice on our behalf, He has raised us up to His level. We are qualified to approach Him because He has made us holy and without blemish by Christ.

In this chapter we will consider the first word in that remarkable phrase in Ephesians 1:4, the word "holy." The priest who approached, under the Law, had to be holy as well as without blemish. Holiness is required to approach God in the Old Testament as well as the New Covenant. God's holiness requires the holiness of His people as a condition of approach. One is not qualified to approach God without holiness. But God has made us qualified in Christ.

Clearing up the translation complications regarding this word, "holy," gives the Bible student much needed assistance. If all this chapter does is clear up the muddle of translations regarding this word, it will be of service.

In the Old Testament, the words, saint, sanctify, sanctification, hallow, holy, and holiness, are translations of the same root word in Hebrew—*qodesh*. In the New Testament these words, saint, sanctify, sanctification, hallow, holy, and holiness are translations of the Greek root—*hagios*.

I would suggest that it would be less confusing for the reader of our English Bibles if one basic English word group was used to translate the Hebrew *qodesh* or the Greek *hagios*. For the sake of consistency and clarity, the English word-group, **holy**, will be used in translating the aforementioned Hebrew and Greek words.[1]

Holiness Defined

A general definition of "holy" is "to separate or to set apart for God."[2] Also, holy is used in the sense of purity.[3] The opposite of holy is unclean, defiled, or common. This definition applies to both Old and New Testaments. As we will see, holiness has one ultimate end. The underlying point and purpose of holiness is approaching and fellowshipping with God.

> Leviticus 20:24-26:
> But I have said unto you, Ye shall inherit their land, and I will give it unto you to possess it, a land that floweth with milk and honey: I *am* the LORD your God, which have **separated** you from *other* people.
> Ye shall therefore put difference between clean beasts and unclean, and between unclean fowls and clean: and ye shall not make your souls abominable by beast, or by fowl, or by any manner of living thing that creepeth on the ground, which I have **separated** from you as unclean.
> And ye shall be **holy** [*qadosh*] unto me: for I the LORD *am* **holy** [*qadosh*], and have **severed** you from *other* people, that ye should be mine.

These verses define the word holy. Holiness is the state whereby God set His people apart for Him. God's people were to be separated or severed from the other nations (Deuteronomy 7:6, 14:2). Additionally, God's people were to be separated from unclean or defiled animals (Deuteronomy 14:3-21). Israel was not to eat of these creatures lest they would become unclean themselves. Limited holiness was available in the Old Testament by works and adherence to the ceremonial laws. In the New Testament, we have complete holiness not by our efforts, but by the work of Christ.

Holiness under the Law

Holiness in the context of approaching and worshipping God is the central subject in much of Leviticus.

> Leviticus 19:2:
> Speak unto all the congregation of the children of Israel, and say unto them, Ye shall be holy [*qadosh*]: for I the LORD your God *am* holy [*qadosh*].

This basic statement is fundamental and applies in both Old and New Testaments. To come to God and have fellowship with Him, holiness is required. Since God is holy, He needs those who approach Him to be holy.

> Leviticus 11:44 and 45:
> For I *am* the LORD your God: ye shall therefore sanctify [*qadesh*] yourselves, and ye shall be holy [*qadosh*]; for I *am* holy [*qadosh*]: neither shall ye defile yourselves with any manner of creeping thing that creepeth upon the earth.
> For I *am* the LORD that bringeth you up out of the land of Egypt, to be your God: ye shall therefore be holy [*qadosh*], for I *am* holy [*qadosh*].

Again, God gives the standard: "be holy, for I am holy." Here, in verse 45, God states the basis of that holiness: "For I am the Lord that brings you out of Egypt." God had delivered them from the slavery of Pharaoh in Egypt. He had redeemed them from bondage (Exodus 15:13). Now they belonged to Him and were to be holy.

> Leviticus 22:32 and 33:
> Neither shall ye profane my holy name; but I will be hallowed [*qadesh*] among the children of Israel: I *am* the LORD which hallow [*qadesh*] you,
> That brought you out of the land of Egypt, to be your God: I *am* the LORD.

Again, God commands holiness in light of the Israelites' redemption out of Egypt. The Lord's redemption of Israel from the land of Egypt meant, in legal terms, that the ownership of Israel is transferred from Pharaoh to God.[4] In the New Testament, our redemption and our sanctification are often associated terms (Ephesians 1:4,7 and I Corinthians 1:30).

Most regard the Book of Leviticus as dull codes, laws, and regulations. For many, reading about sacrificial rites, regulations of the priesthood, dietary and legal codes can grow tiresome. The first seven chapters set up the procedure for how to draw near to God's tabernacle with approach offerings. Then in chapters eight and nine, the priesthood is instituted, after which Aaron and his sons are ordained as priests. Chapter nine ends on a note of triumph and exultation.

> Leviticus 9:22-24:
> And Aaron lifted up his hand toward the people, and blessed them, and came down
> from offering of the sin offering, and the burnt offering, and peace offerings.
> And Moses and Aaron went into the tabernacle of the congregation, and came out, and blessed the people: and the glory of the LORD appeared unto all the people.
> And there came a fire out from before the LORD, and consumed upon the altar the burnt offering and the fat:

which when all the people saw, they shouted, and fell on their faces.

The people shouted and fell on their faces in awe and joy that their God was truly among them. They were thrilled beyond measure because their covenant God was a true and powerful God, not a dead, silent idol like those of all the other nations. The fire's commencement and consummation of the sacrifices was proof positive that God had accepted those sacrifices. That fire, which Israel saw God ignite that day would be kept burning from that point on so it could consume all future offerings. Every tribe or nation had their god or gods. Many had their sacrificial rites, priests, and holy places. Only the God of Israel—the true God—manifested such miraculous wonders to His people. What a day that must have been!

"The Nadab and Abihu Incident"

The next chapter of Leviticus opens with an event so horrifying it must have stunned the whole nation. The sharp and shocking contrast between the exaltation of chapter nine and the anguish of chapter 10 is one of the most jarring in Scripture.

> Leviticus 10:1-3:
> And Nadab and Abihu, the sons of Aaron, took either of them his censer, and put fire therein, and put incense thereon, and offered strange fire before the LORD, which he commanded them not.
> And there went out fire from the LORD, and devoured them, and they died before the LORD.
> Then Moses said unto Aaron, This *is it* that the LORD spake, saying, I will be **sanctified** [*qadesh,* made holy] in them that come nigh me [approach, *qaroub*], and

before all the people I will be glorified. And Aaron held his peace.

The issue at hand, the reason these men met with such dire consequences, is spelled out in this one phrase: ". . .I will be sanctified in them that come nigh me. . ." God said He was to be made holy, or "shown to be holy" The central point here was holiness. Their approach was illegitimate because they brought in "strange fire" rather than the fire God had previously ignited on the altar.

At chapter ten, the whole revelation of Leviticus seems to pivot on this issue of holiness. From this point on, this book concerns itself mainly with the holiness of the priests and the people. The various laws given in the following chapters are for the purpose of facilitating holiness and avoiding another occurrence of the dreadful events of Leviticus 10:1-3.

For example, the next section of Leviticus, chapters 11 through 15 dealing with ceremonial laws, closes with this summary verse:

> Leviticus 15:31:
> Thus shall ye separate the children of Israel from their uncleanness; **that they die not** in their uncleanness, when they defile my tabernacle that *is* among them.

The primary point of the ceremonial laws was to not defile the tabernacle with uncleanness so Israel would not die. The tabernacle was the habitation of God on earth. It was mandatory that those who approached gave due consideration to the holiness required.

Many who have studied the Levitical laws have pointed out the positive effects on health, morals, and culture that they provided Israel. They have also deduced that following these laws kept Israel alive until the Messiah could come. This may be true, but the concern here in Leviticus is to "die not in their uncleanness, when they defile my tabernacle. . ." The overriding concern is not the long term effects of certain undesirable eating or health habits *but* to avoid a repeat of what happened to Aaron's sons.

The opening of the next section of Leviticus, starting in chapter 16, directly addresses the concern of dying in an illegitimate approach. It refers back to chapter 10, where the sons of Aaron defiled the sanctuary with strange fire and met with fatal consequences.

> Leviticus 16:1-3a:
> And the LORD spake unto Moses after the death of the two sons of Aaron, when they offered before the LORD, and died;
> And the LORD said unto Moses, Speak unto Aaron thy brother, that he come not at all times into the holy *place* within the vail before the mercy seat, which is upon the ark; **that he die not**: for I will appear in the cloud upon the mercy seat.
> Thus shall Aaron come into the holy *place*:. . .

Here God addresses exactly how to approach and gives the revelation about the Day of Atonement. The fundamental issue addressed in this section of Leviticus is to approach God as He requires.

> Leviticus 22:9:
> They shall therefore keep mine ordinance, lest they bear sin for it, and die therefore, if they profane it: I the LORD do sanctify [*qadesh*] them.

In the context of the laws concerning the priesthood, the issue of holy behavior to prevent death is brought up. The priest who approached had to be holy or there could be dire consequences. Leviticus 22:9 should be read in light of the death of Aaron's sons in chapter 10.

Only Those who are Holy Can Approach

Whether looking at the Old or New Testament, only those who were holy could approach God. This concept becomes explicit in this record of the rebellion of Korah.

> Numbers 16:1-5:
> Now Korah, the son of Izhar, the son of Kohath, the son of Levi, and Dathan and Abiram, the sons of Eliab, and On, the son of Peleth, sons of Reuben, took men:
> And they rose up before Moses, with certain of the children of Israel, two hundred and fifty princes of the assembly, famous in the congregation, men of renown:
> And they gathered themselves together against Moses and against Aaron, and said unto them, *Ye take* too much upon you, seeing **all the congregation are holy** [*qadosh*], every one of them, and the LORD *is* among them: wherefore then lift ye up yourselves above the congregation of the LORD?
> And when Moses heard *it*, he fell upon his face:
> And he spake unto Korah and unto all his company, saying, Even to morrow the LORD will shew who *are* his, and ***who is* holy** [*qadosh*]; **and will cause *him* to come near** [*qarab*] **unto him:** even *him* whom he hath chosen will he cause to come near [*qarab*] unto him.

The central issue here is who has the holiness to approach God. The underlying point and purpose of holiness is stated explicitly. Only those who are holy can approach God. This is just as true here as it is in Ephesians.

Korah said, "all the congregation is holy." Moses said, "the LORD will shew who *are* his, and *who is* holy; and will cause *him* to come near unto him." The whole point is who has the right to approach God? The holy ones have the right to approach. All others do not possess the right. To enter God's presence one must be holy.

God's Label of Choice for the New Testament Believers

In the Old Covenant given under the billowing smoke of Mt. Sinai, Korah's egalitarian approach got him in a lot of trouble. But under the New Covenant, God's label of choice for the believer is *hagios* or "holy one." *Hagios* is translated in our English bibles as "saint." Almost sixty times in the New Testament God calls His people *hagios*, saints, or more literally, holy ones. Time after time God calls you a saint, a holy one, in His Word. Holy, holy, holy—repeat that 60 times—that is how your Heavenly Father sees you! God's opinion of us should have a big effect. If someone called you "stupid" almost sixty times it would have an effect!

What label do you attach to yourself? How do you define yourself? God sees you as holy. The opinions of others toward us affect us, no matter how hard we try not to allow them to do so. Like it or not, how others respond to us is based on their assessment. People respond to us according to their evaluation. You are hired for a job—or not—according to the employer's assessment of you. In social situations you are accepted, or not, according to someone's impression.

Our Lord and Savior, Jesus Christ, has escorted us into God's presence. What is God's assessment of us? His opinion is that we are holy and without blemish. God's opinion should positively alter the opinion we have of ourselves! When we look in the mirror we should see what God sees—a holy one who is without blemish. This sort of appraisal coming straight from God Almighty should have a huge effect on us. It should have greater impact than the assessment of our peers. God's assessment of us as holy and without blemish certainly has a positive impact on His response to us. He has given us access to the throne of His grace!

The Old Testament stipulation that all must be without blemish to approach God still holds true in the New Testament. Since we are holy and without blemish by the work of Jesus Christ, we have access to God. In the New, just as under the Old, holiness is not an end in itself. One is holy in order to approach. When God calls you holy, His implication is, "there is one qualified to approach into My presence."

We have been "sainted" by Christ's substitutional work on the cross (Hebrews 13:12; Colossians 1:22). Our holiness is not by our work, but of grace. According to the Roman Catholic Church one must be "canonized" to be a saint. The "canon" is their book listing all the saints formally acknowledged by the Vatican.[5] Those entered into that book are formally declared and "canonized" as saints. In Philippians another book is mentioned:

> Philippians 4:3:
> And I intreat thee also, true yokefellow, help those women which laboured with me in the gospel, with Clement also, and *with* other my fellowlabourers, whose names *are* in the book of life.

As saints, your names have been entered into the "book of life." This book is not located in Rome but in the heavenlies with God. You are listed as a saint, a holy one, before God. Before one is "sainted," the Roman Church demands some evidences of miracles done by the person. When you manifest holy spirit, it is evidence of the miracle of all miracles, the new birth.

We are made "holy ones" or saints by the work of our Lord and Savior Jesus Christ, not by some religious denomination here on earth. Being "sainted" by the Vatican will not make you holy before God. Let us now consider the New Testament to see *how* we are made holy.

Two Ways We are Made Holy in the New Testament

Limited holiness in the Old Testament was gained by carrying out the law. In the New Testament we are made holy by God's grace in two ways. First, we are made holy—or "sanctified"—by the sacrificial work of Christ. Second, we are made holy by the holy spirit we received at the new birth. Our holiness or sanctification as sons of God is total and complete.

> Hebrews 13:12:
> Wherefore Jesus also, that he might sanctify [make holy, *hagiazo*] the people with his own blood, suffered without the gate.

We have been made holy by the blood of Christ—the sacrifice of our Lord for us. This verse corresponds to Colossians 1:22:

> Colossians 1:22:
> In the body of his flesh through death, to present you holy [*hagios*] and unblameable [without blemish] and unreproveable in his sight.

We are presented to God as holy and without blemish because of Christ's sacrifice for us.

> II Thessalonians 2:13:
> But we are bound to give thanks alway to God for you, brethren beloved of the Lord, because God hath from the beginning chosen you to salvation through sanctification [*hagiasmos*] of the Spirit and belief of the truth:

"...of the Spirit" is genitive of origin in Greek and could be translated "sanctification originating from the spirit." Genitive of origin in the Greek denotes the cause, source and origin.[6] The cause, source and origin of our holiness is that holy spirit we received when we believed the truth of Romans 10:9.

> Romans 15:16:
> That I should be the minister of Jesus Christ to the Gentiles, ministering the gospel of God, that the offering up of the Gentiles might be acceptable, being sanctified [make holy, *hagiazo*] by the Holy Ghost [*pneuma hagios*].

This verse also gives the second way God has made us holy and acceptable. The last phrase of the verse tells how: by holy spirit. We have been made holy by the holy spirit given unto us in the new birth.

God making the Gentiles holy by holy spirit was an immense change that Peter came to grips with in his visit to the household of Cornelius: "God hath shewed me that I should not call any man common or unclean" (Acts 10:28). The opposite of holiness is uncleanness. When the household of Cornelius spoke in tongues in Acts 10:46, it shocked the other Judean believers who came with Peter.

Speaking in tongues was indisputable proof that they had received holy spirit. They too were holy ones, made holy by holy spirit. These Gentiles did not become holy by legal adherence to the Levitical laws of holiness but by receiving the gift of holy spirit.

The holiness that God has made us to be in Christ staggers the mind of the believer today, just as it did Peter. We are not common or unclean. We have been made holy and cleansed without any blemish by the blood of Christ. Additionally, God has given us the gift of holy spirit to grant access to Him. What a complete salvation has been achieved for us by Christ!

> Ephesians 2:18:
> For through him we both have access by one Spirit unto the Father.

Now we should enter into God's presence boldly with a fearless mind, not with groveling like a sick cringing dog. We are not defiled and diseased. How blind we Christians have been to how holy we are! As we realize the holiness we have in Christ, we can come out of the darkness into the brilliant light of God's Word. We can renew our minds putting "on the new man, created in righteousness and true holiness." Indeed, the act of renewing our minds is living our holiness or "sanctification" as sons of God.

> II Corinthians 6:16-7:1:
> And what agreement hath the temple of God with idols? for ye are the temple of the living God; as God hath said, **I will dwell in them, and walk in *them*; and I will be their God, and they shall be my people**.

> Wherefore come out from among them, and be ye separate, saith the Lord, and touch not the unclean *thing*; and I will receive you,
> And will be a Father unto you, and ye shall be my sons and daughters, saith the Lord Almighty.
> **Having therefore these promises**, dearly beloved, let us cleanse [*katharizō*] ourselves from all filthiness of the flesh and spirit, perfecting holiness [*hagiōsunē*] in the fear of God.

What wonderful promises God gives us here. "I will dwell in them, and walk in *them*; and I will be their God, and they shall be my people." Then II Corinthians 7:1 says, "having therefore these promises, dearly beloved. . ."

Just as with the context of II Corinthians 7:1, we certainly have seen wonderful promises in God's Word concerning what God through Christ has done for us. Now, in light of these promises, this verse exhorts us to "cleanse ourselves from all filthiness of flesh and spirit."[7] We have observed previously that Christ has cleansed us. Now we are told to "cleanse ourselves"—to manifest and live what we have already received spiritually. When Paul says "ourselves," he includes *himself* in this exhortation as well. We, by our own free will, need to renew our minds and live the reality of what Christ has accomplished for us. The phrase "perfecting holiness" is more accurately rendered perform or finish holiness. Renewing our minds is not a sudden event or an enduring accomplishment but a continuous process.

Our Double Dose of Holiness Foreshadowed

The coming Messiah and the accomplishments of that Messiah are foreshadowed in various ways in the Old Testament. The utter totality of our holiness that Christ has achieved for us is no exception. As born again sons of God, we are made holy in two ways: the blood of Christ **and** the holy spirit given to us. This double dose of holiness in the New Covenant was remarkably foreshadowed in the Old.

> Exodus 29:21:
> And thou shalt take of the **blood** that *is* upon the altar, and of the **anointing oil**, and sprinkle *it* upon Aaron, and upon his garments, and upon his sons, and upon the garments of his sons with him: and he shall be hallowed [*qadash*], and his garments, and his sons, and his sons' garments with him.

Two items were sprinkled on Aaron and his sons and their garments: blood from the sacrifice on the altar, and anointing oil. The blood and the oil made them holy. The blood of the sacrifice foreshadowed Christ, our sacrifice, who would be crucified for us. The anointing with oil foreshadowed our anointing with the holy spirit.

> I Peter 1:2:
> Elect according to the foreknowledge of God the Father, through sanctification [*hagiasmos*] of the **Spirit**, unto obedience and sprinkling of the **blood** of Jesus Christ: Grace unto you, and peace, be multiplied.

This opening verse of I Peter, addressed to those who knew the Old Testament, hearkens back to the Mosaic revelation. "Sprinkling of the blood of Jesus Christ" is set in beautiful Levitical terminology—illustrating our purity, our cleansing and our sanctification by the work of Jesus Christ on the tree at Calvary. This verse also mentions our "sanctification of the spirit." "Of the spirit" refers to the new birth and is in the genitive case, indicating cause or origin. The cause or origin of our holiness is the holy spirit received at the time of our new birth. These two verses—one in the Old and one in the New—contain both aspects of our holiness before God as sons. Exodus 29:21 foreshadows the reality to come, and I Peter 1:2 reveals the fully accomplished reality.

Anointed to Serve

As mentioned, the anointing with oil in the Old Testament foreshadowed our anointing with holy spirit.

> II Corinthians 1:21 and 22:
> Now he which stablisheth us with you in Christ, and hath anointed us, *is* God;
> Who hath also sealed us, and given the earnest of the Spirit in our hearts.

God has not anointed us with oil but with holy spirit.

> Acts 10:38:
> How God anointed Jesus of Nazareth with the Holy Ghost and with power: who went about doing good, and healing all that were oppressed of the devil; for God was with him.

Jesus Christ was anointed with the holy spirit and power. He was authorized to operate in God's realm wielding His power. Since our anointing is also by the holy spirit, we are similarly empowered.

The priests of the old Covenant were also anointed, foreshadowing the day when all of God's people would be anointed because of the completed work of Christ.

> Leviticus 8:12:
> And he poured of the anointing oil upon Aaron's head, and anointed him, to sanctify [*qadesh*] him.
>
> Exodus 28:41:
> And thou shalt put them upon Aaron thy brother, and his sons with him; and shalt anoint them, and consecrate them, and sanctify [*qadesh*] them, that they may **minister unto me** in the priest's office.

Both these references speak of the same event: the ordination of the priesthood. For Aaron and his sons to be sanctified, or made holy, they were to be anointed with oil. Afterwards, they could "minister unto me" by approaching God in His tabernacle. Once Aaron and his sons were made holy, they had access to serve.

What defining act made Aaron and his sons holy? They became holy because of anointing. Anointing removed them from the realm of the profane, empowering them to operate in the realm of the sacred. They were now allowed to approach the holy places in the tabernacle and handle the holy things.[8]

What defining act has made us holy? Our anointing by holy spirit in the new birth. We have been removed from the realm of the profane into the sacred. We are *in* this world, but we are not *of* this world. We are empowered to operate in God's realm. As holy ones, we can freely and boldly approach God in prayer. We have access to the power of God; therefore we may minister to God's people.

> I Corinthians 12:7-10:
> But the manifestation of the Spirit is **given to every man** to profit withal. For to one is given by the Spirit the word of wisdom; to another the word of knowledge

by the same Spirit; To another faith by the same Spirit; to another the gifts of healing by the same Spirit; To another the working of miracles; to another prophecy; to another discerning of spirits; to another *divers* kinds of tongues; to another the interpretation of tongues:

These nine manifestations are "given to every" saint. In Galatians 5:22 and 23 nine fruits of the spirit are listed. Both sets of nine can and should be operated by everyone in the Church. Every holy one, after the Day of Pentecost, has access to both the manifestation of the spirit **and** the fruit of the spirit.

Ephesians 2:18 speaks of access by one spirit unto the Father. Indeed, these manifestations of holy spirit, listed in I Corinthians 12, facilitate our access to God. The "utterance manifestations"—speaking in tongues, interpretation of tongues and prophecy— give us access to God's utterances by the spirit. The "revelation manifestations"—word of knowledge, word of wisdom and discerning of spirits—give us access to information by the spirit. The "power manifestations"—faith, miracles and healing—give us access to God's power by the spirit. We who are holy and without blemish have such spectacular access to God and His power.

Our access to God and our empowerment by the holy spirit is entirely by grace because of the work of Jesus Christ. The Mosaic revelation was only a shadow of that which was to come. Let us walk in the grace and gifts He has bestowed upon us until that Day when we are called to our home in heaven. Then we will make our final approach to finally see our Lord Jesus Christ face-to-face.

Notes

1. This other English word group—sanctify, sanctified or sanctification—coming from the Latin word, *sanctus*, can introduce some confusion. As theological terms, these words—sanctify, sanctified or sanctification—have some baggage for those from a conservative Protestant orientation. For those with no doctrinal preconceptions it may not matter in the least. Nevertheless, I prefer the more stark and simple word, "holiness" to the ponderous five-syllable Latin derivative—"sanc-ti-fi-ca-tion." At any rate, we will leapfrog over this translation complication by supplying the Hebrew or Greek in brackets regardless of the English word.

2. Wuest, *Word Studies,* Vol. III, part 2, 31; *Young's Concordance; Companion Bible,* Exodus 3:5 note; Milgrom, *Leviticus 17-22,* 1712. All four scholars define holy as to set apart or separate for God.

3. Jacob Milgrom, *The Anchor Bible, Leviticus 17-22,* 1711. "In the Semitic languages, the concept of "holy" is expressed by the root *qdš*. In Akkadian ...*quddusu* means both to "to purify" and to "consecrate."

4. Milgrom, *The Anchor Bible, Leviticus 1-16,* 688.

5. Webster's Dictionary 1828 edition, s.v. "canon."

6. Bullinger, *Figures of Speech Used in the Bible,* 989-1002.

7. In II Corinthians 7:1 this usage of spirit refers to the mind or more explicitly, the inner life of the mind as opposed to the outer body. (Category 7E in *Walking in God's Power,*® *intermediate class, Student Study Guide*.)

8. Milgrom, says (*Leviticus 1-16,* 554): "In the ancient cultures anointing represented a change in legal status." This fits with the Old Testament where it records the anointing of kings, prophets and priests. Becoming ordained or set as a priest, prophet or king was an immense change in status. What an incredible change in status for us when we were anointed with holy spirit!

9

The Intimacy of Our Approach

We have been defining our status as those who are holy and without blemish before Him in love. In chapter seven, we saw that, whether in the Old or New Covenant, God requires those who approach Him to be without blemish. In Leviticus, both priest and sacrifice had to be without blemish to approach God. Now in the New Testament, we are made without blemish by the sacrifice of Christ.

In chapter eight, we learned—whether in Leviticus or in Ephesians—only those who are holy have the right and privilege to approach God. Thus, to come before God's presence one must be holy. Holiness or "sanctification" in the New Testament was accomplished for us by Christ, our complete Savior. We were made holy by his blood shed for us. Then, in order to bring this magnificent spiritual reality into manifestation in our lives, God gave us holy spirit. These two things—Christ's death on our behalf and the holy spirit received at the new birth—give us incomparable holiness before God. And just so we never forget it, God's label of choice for us is "saints," or more literally "holy ones." In the New Testament, about sixty times God uses the term "holy ones" or saints to refer to His people. The one basic conclusion reached in both previous chapters is that the old views or conceptions we hold of ourselves should be set aside. We should adopt God's view of us as

His holy ones who are without blemish, having full access to Him and His power.

Now we will examine the intimacy of our approach to God as those holy and without blemish. In this chapter, we will uncover one of those rare gems so common in the Book of Ephesians. To see the face-to-face access we have to God, we will need to look at a word in the Greek that is barely noted in most English Bibles.

> Ephesians 1:4:
> According as he hath chosen us in him before the foundation of the world, that we should be holy and without blame **before** [*katenōpion*] him in love:

Katenōpion means directly in front of Him—directly opposite, face-to-face. We are holy and without blemish and directly in the presence of God, face-to-face, *eyeball-to-eyeball*. Translating *katenōpion* as "before" is much too vague, lacking the dynamic emphasis and precision this word *katenōpion* carries in the Greek. Since this word *katenōpion* is not adequately translated or understood in our English versions, we will take a close look at this word and see exactly what it means.

Katenōpion is made up of the prefix *kata,* and *enōpion*. *Enōpion* is from the root word *optomai*, meaning "to see," from which the English word "optics" is derived. *Enōpion* is translated "in the sight of" 16 times in the *King James Version*. Bullinger's *Critical Lexicon and Concordance* defines this word as "being in sight; in one's presence, **face to face**." *Liddell and Scott's Lexicon* also defines *enōpion* as "**face to face**." The word *enōpion* is used over ninety times in the New Testament.

> Luke 1:19:
> And the angel answering said unto him, I am Gabriel, that stand in the presence [*enōpion*] of God; and am sent to speak unto thee, and to shew thee these glad tidings.

The angel Gabriel stands in the presence, in the sight of God—face-to-face.

> Revelation 8:2:
> And I saw the seven angels which stood before [*enōpion*] God; and to them were given seven trumpets.

Like Gabriel, these seven angels stood in the presence, in the sight, of God, face-to-face.

> Luke 4:7 and 8:
> If thou therefore wilt worship [*enōpion*] me, all shall be thine.
> And Jesus answered and said unto him, Get thee behind me, Satan: for it is written, Thou shalt worship the Lord thy God, and him only shalt serve.

While the Greek word, *enōpion*, is used in verse 7, there is no corresponding English word in the *King James Version*. This verse takes on a much more chilling and sinister tone when translated more accurately with the word *enōpion*—"If you therefore will worship me, in my presence, face-to-face, all shall be yours."

> Acts 2:25:
> For David speaketh concerning him, I foresaw the Lord always before my face, [*enōpion*] for he is on my right hand, that I should not be moved:

Here *enōpion* is accurately and beautifully translated "before my face." David saw the Lord "before his face." This is indicative of the closeness with which David walked with God as a servant of the Old Covenant. As sons of God, holy and without blemish, we are before His face in love.

Adding the Greek prefix *"kata"* to *enōpion* gives it an extra emphatic punch. *Katenōpion* means directly opposite; face-to-face; directly in His very sight; directly in front of Him. We are right before God—in His presence, face-to-face.

Thayer defines *katenōpion* as "over against, opposite, **before the face of**, before the presence of." Bullinger defines it as "right over against, right opposite." Alford says *katenōpion* implies a special nearness and dearness to Him.[1]

The word *katenōpion,* although buried in the Greek text, is truly one of the gems of the Book of Ephesians. We are holy and without blemish, face-to-face with God in love. What intimacy! What approach! The sinful human mind balks at such an intimate fellowship with God. We know we are not worthy. Yet this magnificent revelation of Ephesians bulldozes all our natural human insecurities aside. We *are* holy. We *are* without blemish. We *are* right before Him, face-to-face, in love.[2]

Remember Abraham coming before God to intercede for Sodom in Genesis 18? He "stood yet before the Lord," time after time (Genesis 18:22). He finally talked God down to ten people. He *wheeled and dealed* with God. We too can come before God boldly, directly into His presence. The approach offering of our Lord has not set back our relationship with God! We are directly in the presence of

God. We, too, can have open and honest discussions with our heavenly Father.

What intimacy we have with our Heavenly Father! Here, as is so often the case with the truths in Ephesians, the human mind balks. The old sin nature twitches and runs for cover. The religious mind of man hems and haws looking for a flaw. There is no flaw in God's Word. We are holy and without blemish—directly in the presence of God.

The Three Uses of *Katenōpion* in the New Testament

This word, *katenopion,* is used only three times in the Greek text of the New Testament.³

> Ephesians 1:4: ". . .holy and without blame **before *[katenōpion]*** him in love."

> Colossians 1:22: ". . .holy and without blemish and unreproveable **in his sight *[katenōpion]*:"

> Jude 24: "Now unto him that is able to keep you from falling, and to present *you* faultless [without blemish] **before the presence *[katenōpion]*** of his glory with exceeding joy."

Each time *katenōpion* is used, it dramatically states the face-to-face intimate approach we have to God through Christ. Also, the word, *katenōpion,* **always** occurs together with "without blemish" This fits with our conclusion in chapter seven—only those without blemish can approach God. Colossians tells us exactly how we became without blemish.

Colossians 1:22—"A Marvelous Picture of Complete Purity"

> Colossians 1:20-22:
> And, having made peace through the **blood of his cross**, by him to reconcile all things unto himself; by him, *I say*, whether *they be* things in earth, or things in heaven.
> And you, that were sometime alienated and enemies in *your* mind by wicked works, yet now hath he reconciled
> In the **body of his flesh** through death, to present you holy and unblameable [without blemish, *amōmos*] and unreproveable in his sight:

Throughout the entire Bible, the two central elements of sacrifice are blood and flesh. In this passage, these elements of sacrifice are mentioned. The "blood of his cross" (v.20) and "the body of his flesh through death" (v. 22) are paralleled, pointing to Christ's complete sacrifice for us.

The words "blood of his cross" stand out because of the figure of speech, metonymy. The figure, metonymy, occurs when there is an <u>exchange of one noun for a related noun</u>. For example, we may say, "the White House said today. . ." Did the White House literally talk? No, the people in the White House spoke. This is a metonymy. The noun, White House, is exchanged for a related noun—the <u>people</u> in the White House.[4]

We may use figures haphazardly or unknowingly, but the Word of God—written by holy men of God as they were moved by the Holy Spirit—uses them with deliberate accuracy and precision. Two common examples of the figure metonymy, from the Scriptures, are "speaking in tongues" and "for God so loved the world." Tongues is, literally, "languages" and in John 3:16, God did not love the physical earth but the people living on it.

E. W. Bullinger in his book, *Figures of Speech used in the Bible*, shows how the word, "blood" is actually a "double metonymy." The word "cross" is also a "double metonymy."[5] Here, in Colossians 1:20, the terms "blood" of Christ or the "cross" of Christ both refer to his death as distinct from his life. That is, instead of simply saying "death," God's Word uses a related noun, "blood." Instead of saying "crucifixion," God's Word says "cross." Using the word "blood" is more emphatic and vivid. Using the word "cross," the instrument of Christ's execution, gives more emphasis and catches the attention of the reader.

However, there is an additional metonymy. The death of Christ here in Colossians, represented by "blood" and "cross," is not just a reference to the historical event of the crucifixion of our Lord. Rather, the death of Christ refers to <u>what his death accomplished</u>. His blood is put for his death and in turn, by metonymy, his death is put for his accomplishments. Also, the cross refers to his death, and then in turn, for what his death achieved—our complete redemption and salvation.

Here is another example of this double metonymy: "enemies of the cross of Christ" (Philippians 3:18). The <u>cross,</u> by metonymy, refers to the related noun—the <u>death</u> of Christ. Are there enemies of the actual historical event of the death of Christ? No, unbelievers the world over have no problem with Jesus of Nazareth dying an ignominious death on the cross. So, what are they opposing? What are they enemies of? They would deny that Jesus Christ's death accomplished our redemption and salvation. Here, the cross, the instrument of Christ's death is put for his death.

And then Christ's death, by metonymy, is put for what his death accomplished; hence it is a "double metonymy."

The expression "blood of his cross" could be called "double-double" metonymy. The word "blood" and the word "cross" are both double metonymies in and of themselves. "Blood of his cross" is one "super-metonymized" phrase with a supersized emphasis.

Colossians 1:20 also says, "And having made peace through the blood of his cross, by him to reconcile all things unto himself. . ." One of the colossal accomplishments of Christ's death was to bring God's people peace and reconciliation.

Our reconciliation and peace with God, by the sacrifice of Jesus Christ, is powerfully foreshadowed by the Old Testament peace offering (Leviticus 3; 7:11-36). The peace offering was the only offering in the Old Testament where a portion of the sacrifice was returned to the offerer. A part was given to the priest and then a part was given to God to be burnt on the altar. Unlike other offerings, all three parties (the offerer, the priest, and God) shared a portion of the peace offering. Each partook of the offering. This mutual partaking represented a full sharing and reconciliation with God, the priest and the offerer. The offerer would take his portion and sit down to a fellowship meal with this family and friends. In eating the peace offering, the offerer and those who dined with him, fully identified with all that the offering and the altar represented. This offering formed a touching picture of reconciliation, fellowship and harmony between God and His people. (See Appendix B on the peace offering.)

The sacrifice of Christ brought this harmonious picture into full reality. We are full partakers in all that Christ achieved. We are at peace with God and with each other. We are reconciled to God, basking in fellowship with God and with one another. "Made nigh [near] by the blood of Christ. For his is our peace [offering], who hath made both one..." (Ephesians 2:13a-14b).

Colossians 1:22 also mentions that we are "unreproveable in his sight." The word "unreprovable"—*anegkletous* in Greek—is not mentioned in Ephesians 1:4. Clearly as Christians we are not "unreprovable" since II Timothy 3:16 says the purpose of the Word of God is for "reproof". A better translation from the Greek of this word is unaccusable or unimpeachable. According to Robertson, in the secular Greek this word is used when after a public accounting or an examination to find flaws or faults is complete, none are found. After such a thorough examination, the person would be declared *anegkletous*—"unaccusable" or "unimpeachable."[6]

We are "unaccusable in His sight"—*anegkletous katenopion*! Directly in the very presence of God we are unaccusable! These are words which should shake the believer down to the very depths of his heart. We know we are sinners, and our salvation is truly by grace. Our Lord Jesus Christ has accomplished for us what was utterly unthinkable on our own.

Robertson describes these three words in Colossians 1:22—holy, unblemished and unimpeachable—"as giving a marvelous picture of complete purity (positive and negative, internal and external)."[7] What a complete work our Lord and Savior has done on our behalf! Since we are so completely pure in God's sight, we can come before His very presence without any sense of sin, guilt or shortcomings.

Jude 24—Our Presentation in Glory

At the Return of Christ for His Church, God's ultimate desire and plans will be fulfilled. This will be our final approach into God's presence. We will stand with new bodies before Him, face-to-face. At this time, we will receive the full realization of our access to Him.

> Jude 24:
> Now unto him that is able to keep you from falling, and to present *you* faultless [without blemish, *amōmos*] before the presence [*katenōpion*] of his glory with exceeding joy.

Our presentation before God by Christ in glory will be with exceeding joy. Our presentation in heaven will be as we have been on earth—holy and without blemish.

This short Book of Jude warns of the loss of the right way of believing. It is an exhortation to strenuously contend for and to remember the Word of God (v. 3,5,17). The body of the epistle, verses 3-23, exhorts a return to God's Word. In contrast, the opening greeting and the closing doxology speak of what God has done through Christ.

> Opening:
>
> Jude 1 and 2:
> Jude, the servant of Jesus Christ, and brother of James, to them that are sanctified by God the Father, and preserved in Jesus Christ, *and* called:
> Mercy unto you, and peace, and love, be multiplied.

Closing:

Jude 24 and 25:
Now unto him that is able to keep you from falling, and to present *you* faultless [without blemish, *amōmos*] before the presence of his glory with exceeding joy,
To the only wise God our Saviour, *be* glory and majesty, dominion and power, both now and ever. Amen.

The opening and closing verses in Jude serve as bookends and speak of God's accomplished work in Christ. Whether people choose to maintain God's truth in their lives or not, His peace and love are still multiplied. Some may turn against the right way of believing, but His glory, majesty, dominion and power are still a reality now and forever. Right now, in this present evil world, God is able to keep us from falling. And God is able at the Gathering Together to present us without blemish in glory with exceeding joy. This will be our final, glorious approach to God by our Lord Jesus Christ.

I Corinthians 13:9-12:
For we know in part, and we prophesy in part.
But when that which is perfect [*teleion*, complete, full grown, mature] is come, then that which is in part shall be done away.
When I was a child, I spake as a child, I understood as a child, I thought as a child: but when I became a man, I put away childish things.
For now we see through a glass, darkly; but then face to face: now I know in part; but then shall I know even as also I am known.

"But when that which is perfect is come. . ." refers to the Second Coming of Christ as Jude 24 mentions. The Greek has the definite article, "when **the perfect** is come. . ."

What a magnificent comparison! It should be noted that the mirrors of the Bible times were highly polished metal. The metal was quick to tarnish and had surface imperfections. Therefore, "seeing though a glass darkly" had meaning to the Corinthians. The inference of this expression is that we only see and understand obscurely. However, at the Gathering Together of the Church we shall see clearly, face-to-face.

"But then shall I know [future, at the Return] even as also I am known [present, right now]." How are we known by God **right now**? Are we seen as miserable sinners, unholy and flawed, with God looking on in disgust? I trust that after our recent examination of Ephesians 1:4 we can set those notions aside!

God knows with perfect clarity that we are His masterpieces in Christ, holy and without blemish. We are now lovingly in His sight, face-to-face. We have total access to Him. God knows us in all things. I John 3:20 says, "For if our heart condemn us, God is greater than our heart, and knoweth all things." God knows what He has done for us in Christ.

For us to live our lives with fear and self-loathing is to reject what God clearly states in His Word. Romans 8:1 says, "There is therefore now no condemnation to them which are in Christ Jesus." We are released from the bondage of condemnation.

Romans 8:15-18:

For ye have not received the spirit of bondage again to fear; but ye have received the

Spirit of adoption [sonship], whereby we cry, Abba, Father.

The Spirit itself beareth witness with our spirit, that we are the children of God:

And if children, then heirs; heirs of God, and joint-heirs with Christ; if [since] so be that we suffer with *him,* that we may be also glorified together.

For I reckon that the sufferings of this present time *are* not worthy *to be compared* with the glory which shall be revealed in us.

While we are now holy and without blemish, face-to-face before Him in love, there is no comparison to what shall be revealed in future glory. There is absolutely no meaningful correspondence or resemblance between the present time and the glory that shall be revealed in us. We have not yet received the full realization of our sonship. But there is a day coming when all of God's plans for His Church will be brought to completion. Then our full and final approach unto God in the heavenlies will come to pass. What a day of glory that will be!

Notes

1. Wuest, *Word Studies*, Volume 1, Ephesians, 34.

2. "In love" could perhaps be placed as the opening of verse 5; however, in this study we will leave "in love" with verse 4. Lightfoot notes that the words "in love" stand <u>after</u> the phrase to which they belong. For example, Ephesians 3:17; 4:2, 15, 16; 5:2 and Colossians 2:2. [J. B. Lightfoot, *Notes on Epistles of St. Paul* (Grand Rapids, MI: Baker, reprinted 1980), 313.] Regardless of where "in love" is placed—with verse 4 or verse 5— love is the Father's main motive and primary cause. God's love is "the great primary cause of all causes" (Welch, 74).

3. The Stephen's Greek text places *katenōpion* in II Corinthians 2:17 and 12:19; however, critical Greek texts Lachmann, Tischendorf, Tregelles and Alford place the word *katenanti* in place of *katenōpion* in II Corinthians 2:17 and 12:19. See Bullinger's *Lexicon* Preface for an explanation of these various Critical Greek texts.

4. Much of my explanation is from, or indebted to, Walter Cummins [*Scripture Conference, An Introduction to Figures of Speech*, 1995, 16.]

5. Bullinger, *Figures of Speech,* 610-12. He explains how the words blood and cross are both a *Metalepsis* or Double Metonymy. Bullinger's comments are as relevant today as when he wrote them, about one hundred years ago:

> Col. 1:20.—"And, having made peace through the blood of his cross." Here again, "cross" is put for

his death, and His death is put for all its meritorious results.

It is by forcing the word "cross" into a literal meaning in such passages as the above that the Church of Rome has appeared to have a Scriptural sanction for its reverence for, and adoration of, "the cross."

The reader may easily see where the word "cross" is used literally and historically and where it is used figuratively. If the latter be substituted for the former, not only shall we introduce much error, but we shall lose much of precious Scriptural truth and teaching.

6. Robertson, *Word Pictures*, Vol. IV, p. 482.

7. Robertson, *Word Pictures*, Vol. IV, p. 482.

10

The Final Approach

The final leg of an airliner's journey is often called the "final approach." The final leg of our journey toward an eternity in God's presence may also be called the "Final Approach."

> I Thessalonians 4:13-18:
> But I would not have you to be ignorant, brethren, concerning them which are asleep, that ye sorrow not, even as others which have no hope.
> For if we believe that Jesus died and rose again, even so them also which sleep in Jesus will God bring with him.
> For this we say unto you by the word of the Lord, that we which are alive *and* remain unto the coming of the Lord shall not prevent them which are asleep.
> For the Lord himself shall descend from heaven with a shout, with the voice of the archangel, and with the trump of God: and the dead in Christ shall rise first:
> Then we which are alive *and* remain shall be caught up together with them in the clouds, to meet the Lord in the air: and so shall we ever be with the Lord.
> Wherefore comfort one another with these words.

These verses elaborate the final approach of the Church to enjoy eternity in God's presence. Verse 17 concludes, "and so shall we ever be with the Lord." In presence of God and our Lord Jesus Christ, we will reside and display the exceeding riches of His grace for all eternity. God's utmost desire is to be with His people, to have full fellowship with them. At the glorious Gathering Together, on the ascension day of the Church, we shall dwell eternally before our Heavenly Father's face.

What a joyful day that will be! The physical separation from beloved ones in the Body of Christ, caused by distance or death, will be gone. The sense of detachment we have had from our Lord Jesus Christ and from those who have fallen asleep will be ended forever. This reality, our hope, is indeed one of the great comforts in this life.

Laying Hold on the Hope

> Hebrews 6:18-20:
> That by two immutable things, in which *it was* impossible for God to lie, we might have a strong consolation, who have fled for refuge to lay hold upon the hope set before us:
> Which *hope* we have as an anchor of the soul, both sure and stedfast, and which entereth into that within the veil;
> Whither the forerunner [*prodromos*] is for us entered, *even* Jesus, made an high priest for ever after the order of Melchisedec.

A *prodromos* is one who comes in advance where the rest will follow. Christ as the *prodromos* has opened up a new route of access from earth to heaven. He was the first to traverse this new route by way of his ascension. At the trumpet blast of the Gathering Together, this route will be open for the final approach of the Church of Grace into the heavenlies—to the inner sanctum of heaven. We are presented "faultless before the presence of his glory with exceeding joy" (Jude 24). The fullness of God's desire will be brought to pass. This is the "hope set before us" of Hebrew 6:18.

This passage in Hebrews six holds a remarkable illustration—the hope is called an "anchor of the soul." The anchor, though not visible, secures a ship to keep it from drifting. As we stay anchored to the hope of Christ's Return, we are not carried along by the currents of this world, wafted by the force of circumstance.

While this chapter is titled "The Final Approach," to signify the end of a journey by air, the anchor may offer a similar parallel in sea travel. Travelers by ship lower an anchor when nearing land (Acts 27:29 and 30). The imagery suggested by Hebrews 6:19 is that our hope has already been secured at the port of destination. We are no longer in danger of being lost in the currents and storms of the open sea.[1] Our harbor of destination has been secured. The anchor holds sure and steadfast. Now we must fasten this reality in our minds.

There is a most striking parallel found in the secular Greek. The word *prosagōgē*— translated "access" in Romans 5:2, Ephesians 2:18 and 3:12 has various usages in the Greek. In other words, this word is used in different ways with different definitions. As we saw in chapter four, the primary definition of *prosagōgē* involves an escorted introduction to the royal presence.

However, there is another usage or definition of this word *prosagōgē* in the secular Greek: a haven for ships, a safe harbor, was called a *prosagōgē*. Plutarch speaks of an army waiting on shore where there was no *prosagōgē* —no place for ships to harbor safely. In Sophecles, the question is posed: "what need made you put in (*prosagō*) to Lemnos?"[2] So *prosagōgē* is an approach to land, a secure harbor, a safe place to put in a ship.

". . .We have access [*prosagōgē*] by faith into this grace wherein we stand. . ." (Romans 5:2). We have safe haven, secure anchorage and access to God.

> Psalm 107:29 and 30:
> He maketh the storm a calm, so that the waves thereof are still.
> Then are they glad because they be quiet; so he bringeth them unto their desired haven.

The desired haven of our lives is the quiet fellowship we have with our heavenly Father. We have *prosagōgē*—safe harbor—to God by our Lord Jesus Christ.

When a loved one dies, one is often advised to work to "face the reality" of the finality of death. Accepting one's loss is referred to as the "grieving process." Psychological professionals say the human mind has only a limited capacity to grasp the totality of death; therefore, it must be absorbed step-by-step. What professionals generally refer to as the stages of the grieving process are as follows: denial, anger, forgiveness, and acceptance. While understanding this process may be helpful, in contrast, God's Word details a *"growth process."*

> Hebrews 6:11 and 12a:
> And we desire that every one of you do shew the same diligence to the full assurance of hope unto the end: that ye be not slothful,. . .

Hebrews 6:11 refers to a "growing process" that should be undertaken by **every** believer with all diligence. "Every one of you do shew the same diligence to the full assurance of hope. . ." God's Word advises "every one of you" to exert the time and effort needed to get to the point of "full assurance" when it comes to the hope. Wuest's translation reads:

> Hebrews 6:11 and 12a:
> But we are strongly desirous that each one of you exhibit the same diligence which will develop your hope into full assurance until the end, in order that you may become not sluggish. . .

Serious effort should be given to "develop your hope into full assurance. . ." Getting to the point of full assurance or total persuasion takes development. God's Word lays out steps in the *"growing process"* that every one of us should undertake. Apparently, the human mind has a great capacity to be a dullard in developing this full persuasion of the hope. Here God's Word exhorts us to give diligence to absorb the reality of our hope.

The first step in this *"growing process"* is to recognize that **God is faithful to His Word. It is impossible for God to lie** (Hebrews 6:18). God's Word has immutable integrity. God's Word *will* come to pass. We must grasp the finality and authority of God's Word.

Next, effort must be taken to lay hold onto the hope of Christ's Return. This laying hold is not a passive acknowledgment; to "lay hold" is to seize onto the reality of Christ's return. The hope is sure and steadfast because of the impossibility of God's unfaithfulness to His Word. For this reason, we are to flee "for refuge to lay hold upon the hope set before us." Since it is impossible for God to lie, we are to anchor our souls into the Hope—to hold fast to the actuality of Christ's return. To lay hold on to the hope is not mental assent or a passing consideration of a few Bible verses. No—it is a vigorous act of the mind to grasp the immutable reality of the Lord's return. The Lord Jesus Christ was crucified, resurrected and ascended through the heavenlies. One day he will return for his church; and upon his return, we will follow him to our home in the heavens.

We must recognize the truth that we have a high priest who has entered within the veil of God's inner sanctum in heaven. This is not into some earthly sanctuary built by human hands, but into heaven itself. Our Lord is not only high priest but "forerunner" as well. A forerunner is one who goes in advance where the rest will follow. Jesus Christ promised, "...I will come again, and receive you unto myself; that where I am, *there* ye may be also" (John 14:3).

In order to "lay hold" on the hope, we need to go to the Word of God to build this in our minds. The following passages help us gain more accurate knowledge of the Lord's return. This information aids the "*growing process*" of laying hold onto the hope with full assurance.

> Philippians 3:20 and 21:
> For our conversation is in heaven; from whence also we look for the Saviour, the Lord Jesus Christ:
> Who shall change our vile body, that it may be fashioned like unto his glorious body, according to the working whereby he is able even to subdue all things unto himself.

The "vile body" is literally "lowly body." Our "lowly" body is formed out of the dust of the ground (Genesis 2:7). It is from the earth. At the Gathering Together, we get a glorious new body like the one that Christ received at his resurrection.

> I Corinthians 15:48-50:
> As *is* the earthy, such *are* they also that are earthy: and as *is* the heavenly, such *are* they also that are heavenly.
> And as we have borne the image of the earthy [Adam], we shall also bear the image of the heavenly [Christ].
> Now this I say, brethren, that flesh and blood cannot inherit the kingdom of God; neither doth corruption inherit incorruption.

These verses answer the problem posed in I Corinthians 15:35: "How are the dead raised up? and with what body do they come?" This passage addresses this age-old question. Verse 50 says our natural bodies of flesh and blood never make it to heaven. But our spiritual body—"the image of the heavenly"—will! (verse 49).

> I Corinthians 15:51-55:
> Behold, I shew you a mystery; We shall not all sleep, but we shall all be changed,
> In a moment, in the twinkling of an eye, at the last trump: for the trumpet shall sound, and the dead shall be raised incorruptible, and we shall be changed.
> For this corruptible must put on incorruption, and this mortal *must* put on immortality.
> So when this corruptible shall have put on incorruption, and this mortal shall have put on immortality, then shall be brought to pass the saying that is written, Death is swallowed up in victory.
> O death, where *is* thy sting? O grave, where *is* thy victory?

How final is death? How permanent is death? Death which is so feared, the cause of so much sorrow, is on thin ice at this late hour. A day is coming when death will be non-existent. Death's grip, the wintry permafrost of the soul, will thaw. Our Lord will beam from the portals of heaven in all brilliance. Death will be swallowed up in victory. Death will be destroyed (I Corinthians 15:26).

The regime of death that has been in place since the Fall of Adam and Eve, will be overthrown. As God's Word puts it: "death is swallowed up in victory. The victory is to "ever be with the Lord"—to be basking in His presence for all eternity. This is God's foremost desire: to be with His people.

The Sinai Approach and the Zion Approach

There are two great mountains recorded in Scripture: Sinai and Zion. Both have tremendous significance figuratively and geographically. The location of Mt. Sinai is in question. It could be in Arabia or on the Sinai Peninsula. However, one of the most important facts of Biblical geography is the location of Mt. Zion. Mt. Zion is located at Jerusalem. Therefore, Mt. Zion is often synonymous with the city of Jerusalem in its Biblical usage.[3]

Mt. Sinai is where Moses received the Law from God by revelation. Mt. Sinai, therefore, has come to represent the Law and the Old Covenant. Aaron was installed as high priest at Mt. Sinai. Here the system of priesthood, sacrifice, and the tabernacle under the Old Covenant, was established.

On a hill just outside Jerusalem, Christ died and inaugurated a new covenant, which completely closed out the Law. When Hebrews 6:20 refers to Christ as "an high priest for ever after the order of Melchisedec," it is especially important to recognize that Melchisedec was the priest and king of the ancient city of Jerusalem (Genesis 14:18). Hebrews explains how the priesthood of Christ relates to Melchisedec out of Jerusalem, not Aaron out of Sinai.

In Hebrews 12, these two mountains are used to explicitly illustrate the two different approaches to God—the "Sinai Approach" and the "Zion Approach."

> Hebrews 12:18-24:
> **For ye are not come** [approach, *proserkomai*] unto the mount [Sinai] that might be touched, and that burned with fire, nor unto blackness, and darkness, and tempest,
> And the sound of a trumpet, and the voice of words; which *voice* they that heard intreated that the word should not be spoken to them any more:
> (For they could not endure that which was commanded, And if so much as a beast touch the mountain, it shall be stoned, or thrust through with a dart:
> And so terrible was the sight, *that* Moses said, I exceedingly fear and quake:)
> **But ye are come** [approach, *proserkomai*] unto mount Sion [Zion], and unto the city of the living God, the heavenly Jerusalem, and to an innumerable company of angels,
> To the general assembly and church of the firstborn, which are written in heaven, and to God the Judge of all, and to the spirits of just men made perfect,
> And to Jesus the mediator of the new covenant, and to the blood of sprinkling, that speaketh better things than *that* of Abel.

With the "Sinai Approach," even Moses, who knew God face-to-face, said, "I exceedingly fear and quake." The people of Israel pleaded for Moses to shoulder the responsibility of approaching God. As we saw in chapter eight, under Sinai's shadow, Korah's rash approach brought about his destruction (Numbers 16:27-33). Under Sinai, Aaron's sons were also destroyed for their illegitimate approach with "strange fire."[4] Under Sinai—with only types and shadows of the coming redeemer—God could not allow free approach to Him. If just anyone could have strutted into God's presence under the Old Covenant, Christ, The Way into God's presence, would not have been necessary.

Our approach to God is not the "Sinai approach" but the "Zion approach." This approach to Mt. Zion is the final approach for all God's people.

> Hebrews 12:22-24:
> **But ye are come [approach,** *proserkomai*] unto mount Sion [Zion], and unto the city of the living God, the heavenly Jerusalem, and to an innumerable company of angels,
> To the general assembly and church of the firstborn, which are written in heaven, and to God the Judge of all, and to the spirits of just men made perfect,
> And to Jesus the mediator of the new covenant, and to the blood of sprinkling, that speaketh better things than *that* of Abel.

"But ye **are** come. . ." is an absolute future reality that is stated in the present tense to emphasize the certainty of this future event. This figure of speech, often used in the Bible, is called *Heterosis* of the tense: one tense is exchanged for another. The literal truth of Hebrews 12:22 is that we are—

in the future—going to the heavenly Jerusalem. This immutable reality is so certain that God puts it in the present tense—"ye **are** come."[5] What a wonderful figure of speech which draws our attention to and intensifies the immutability of God's promises!

When verse 22 speaks of "the city of the living God, the heavenly Jerusalem," it refers the city of Revelation 21 and 22. Before these two closing chapters of the Bible, the "heavenly Jerusalem" is only written of prophetically. The heavenly city is not available and does not exist until Revelation 21. Some have understood the heavenly Jerusalem to be a general term for heaven itself; however, the Scriptures are clear that this City of the living God occurs in the future. Hebrews 13:14 says "we have no continuing city, but we see one **to come**." The Gathering Together of the Church (I Thessalonians 4:13-18) as well as the events of Revelation must come to pass before the heavenly Jerusalem is established.

Our resplendent approach into this future heavenly Jerusalem is an absolute certainty and guaranteed reality. Our ascent to this heavenly city is not by our own works and power but by what Christ has already accomplished for us at Calvary.

Hebrews 12:23 opens with a rather vague rendering of the Greek text: "To the general assembly. . ." This phrase is one Greek word, *panēguris*. This word appears only once in the Greek New Testament. When a word is only used once in the New Testament, it is often helpful to examine outside secular usages of the word. This is particularly the case with the word *panēguris* since it has such a vivid and unique depth of meaning.

The basic definition of *panēguris*, in Greek, is a festival, a joyful gathering to celebrate a formal occasion. Wuest renders it as follows: "In festal, joyful gathering or sacred festival." The word *panēguris* was used of the sacred festivals of the Greek Olympic games. The national gatherings for the Olympic games were celebrations with great joy; it was a jubilant time of the celebration of victory and the bestowing of rewards and crowns to the competitors.[6] Moreover, these sacred festivals were solemn and sacred events involving religious acts with priests and sacrifices.

Hebrews 12 opens with an athletic expression which exhorts us to "run with patience the race." In verse 22, the word *panēguris* continues the thought by evoking the glory and joy in store for the victors within the heavenly city. The *panēguris* is where the whole assembly celebrates the victory of the garlanded competitors.[7]

Verse 23 continues: ". . .and church of the firstborn, which are written in heaven." The text reads, "church of firstborn ones."[8] Again, here in Hebrews, the Old Testament is applied to New Testament truth. In the Old Testament, the firstborn belonged to God.[9] This was the case because all the firstborn of Israel had been redeemed by the blood of the Passover lamb. Therefore, all the firstborn of man or beast was owned by God. In the New Testament the "Church of the firstborn" refers back to the Old Testament truth. Those who are redeemed by the blood of the Passover lamb, belong to God. We were redeemed by Christ, our Passover lamb; therefore, now we belong to God.

"The firstborn" also implies the right of inheritance and blessing. Deuteronomy 21:17 mentions the special "right of the firstborn" and that he receives a double portion.

Esau, the firstborn, referenced in Hebrews 12:16, sold his birthright. The inheritance and blessing of the firstborn went to his younger brother, Jacob. As the "church of firstborn ones" we are joint heirs with Christ (Romans 8:17).

The next phrase in Hebrews 12:23, "written in heaven" could be stated more accurately as, "registered in heaven." In the ancient world, registration established one's identity as a citizen.[10] We have full citizenship in the heavenly Jerusalem. Philippians 4:3 also mentions a "book of life" wherein the names of the saints are written. This book is not on this earth. The book of life is not in some vault that can be opened and your name expunged. No, this book is in heaven where no human hands can reach to blot it out.

". . .And to God the Judge of all" emphasizes that all stand before God and give an account. The judgement of men will carry no weight whatsoever; only God's opinion will matter. In the context of Hebrews, this judgement is often positive. This reality stands in stark contrast to the society in which these faithful Hebrew believers lived. They had suffered persecution, shame, and the plunder of their material possessions. Hebrews 10:34 says they "took joyfully the spoiling of your goods, knowing in [for] yourselves that ye have in heaven a better and an enduring substance." In heaven, these believers will receive back something greater and more enduring. God, as judge, will see that all is set right.

Hebrews 12:23 closes with, ". . .and to the spirits of just men made perfect." The usage of the word spirit in this context is best understood as, "the spirit nature of resurrected man."[11] "Made perfect" means made complete in resurrection (Hebrews 11:35b and 40).

Hebrews 12:24 concludes this profound section of God's Word: "And to Jesus the mediator of the new covenant, and to the blood of sprinkling, that speaketh better things than *that* of Abel." This completes the depiction of the great final approach of all God's people into the heavenly city.

In Hebrews, Christ's function as mediator—one who stands in the middle—includes his dual-role as our sacrifice and our high priest. His priestly mediation is not only to intercede on our behalf (7:25) but also, by means of his death, to completely cleanse us from all sin (9:14 and 15). Finally, as our mediator of the new covenant, he provides us access to the heavenly city. What a complete Savior!

The sprinkling of the blood of a sacrifice relates to both cleansing and covenant making. The sacrifice of our Lord Jesus Christ paid the price for our total cleansing **and** our approach unto our heavenly home. There is no approach to God without cleansing. Our final approach has been made possible by the work of Christ as our high priest and sacrifice.

Hebrews 12:24 ends with, ". . .and to the blood of sprinkling**, that speaketh better things than** *that* **of Abel**." This final phrase is most striking. First, mentioning Abel engulfs almost the whole span of Scripture. As we bathe in the truths of the heavenly Jerusalem, the mention of Abel wrenches us back to the opening pages of the Bible, to a dreadful murder. Also startling is the statement that the blood of Christ "speaketh." Since Christ's blood "speaketh better things" than that of Abel's blood, of what did Abel's blood speak? In Genesis 4 God addresses Cain after he murdered his brother Abel.

Genesis 4:10 and 11:
And he [God] said, What hast thou done? the voice of thy brother's blood crieth unto me from the ground.
And now *art* thou cursed from the earth, which hath opened her mouth to receive thy brother's blood from thy hand;

Cain replies:

Genesis 4:14, 16:
. . .Behold, thou hast driven me out this day from the face of the earth; and **from thy face shall I be hid**; and I shall be a fugitive and a vagabond in the earth; and it shall come to pass, *that* every one that findeth me shall slay me.

And Cain went out from the presence of the LORD, and dwelt in the land of Nod, on the east of Eden.

This account ties in with our great subject of Jesus Christ our approach offering. For shedding the blood of Abel, Cain was driven out from the presence of God. The blood of Abel cried out from the earth for vengeance and estrangement from God. Cain was driven out from God's face and became a fugitive. But the blood of Christ speaks of better things than that of Abel. While the blood of Abel cried out for judgement and enmity, the blood of Christ speaks of forgiveness and reconciliation. The blood of Abel drove Cain from the presence of God. But by the blood of Jesus, we are brought into the very presence of God.

The Heavenly Jerusalem: Revelation 21 and 22

Revelation 21 and 22 speaks of the promised "new heaven and earth," coming to pass. This is "the city of the living God, the heavenly Jerusalem" mentioned in Hebrews 12:22.

> Revelation 21:1-4:
> And I saw a new heaven and a new earth: for the first [former] heaven and the first [former] earth were passed away; and there was no more sea.
> And I John saw the holy city, new Jerusalem, coming down from God out of heaven, prepared as a bride adorned for her husband.
> And I heard a great voice out of heaven saying, Behold, the tabernacle of God *is* with men, and he will dwell with them, and they shall be his people, and God himself shall be with them, *and be* their God.
> And God shall wipe away all tears from their eyes; and there shall be no more death, neither sorrow, nor crying, neither shall there be any more pain: for the former things are passed away.

At this time, all the books will have been closed on heaven and earth as we know it. The heaven and earth that we now live in will have been completely obliterated. The great Gathering Together of the Church of I Thessalonians 4:13-18 as well as the events of Revelation will have transpired. The judgements of both the just and unjust of Revelation 20 will be over. Now, here in the closing two chapters of the Bible, a completely new eon opens. Revelation 21 and 22 describe in vivid detail this new age.

Revelation 21:3 declares God's will for this new age: "And I heard a great voice out of heaven saying, Behold, the tabernacle of God *is* **with** men, and he will dwell **with** them, and they shall be his people, and God himself shall be **with** them, *and be* their God."

Since this is the very first declaration made upon the inception of this brand new heaven and earth, it follows that this is the founding operative principle of this new age. Now God's utmost desire of all ages becomes a complete reality—His people are **with** Him. This is far beyond the "final approach." This is a new age, a new heaven, a new earth, with the fundamental purpose of God dwelling with His people, with total access and approach to Him. Total reconciliation with His people is the accomplished reality of this new age.

> Revelation 21:4:
> And God shall wipe away all tears from their eyes; and there shall be no more death, neither sorrow, nor crying, neither shall there be any more pain: for the former things are passed away.

All the consequences of the fall of Lucifer and the sin of Adam are wiped away. The devastation and the disruption caused by these cataclysmic events are utterly terminated. Death itself is abolished. Now that's closure! We can bask in the absolute certainty that this Word of God will come to pass.

Christ's redemptive work extends beyond the Church, beyond us to the whole of creation, the whole universe. As Romans 8:22 says, "the whole creation groaneth and travaileth in pain together until now." With the events of Revelation 21 and 22, there will come a new heaven and a new earth. Christ's redemptive work includes the entire creation.

This new heaven and earth is constructed to facilitate God's final desire—to dwell with His people for all eternity. To further portray God's intense desire to be with His people, the illustration of the bride and bridegroom is used:

> Revelation 21:2:
> And I John saw the holy city, new Jerusalem, coming down from God out of heaven, prepared as a bride adorned for her husband.

This verse illustrates the total intimacy and delight between God and His people, who will abide together forever. What a beautiful illustration!

But there is a more dominant symbol in these final chapters of the Word of God: the symbol used for our Lord Jesus Christ. Seven times in these closing two chapters of Revelation our Lord is referred to as "the Lamb."[12] Throughout Scripture, Christ has a multitude of titles, but here he is called "the Lamb." The significance of this final symbol of Christ in the Word of God can hardly be overstated.

What does this symbolic title represent? Why refer to our wonderful Lord and Savior as the "lamb"? While some of the symbols of Revelation are puzzling, this one is clearly explained the first time it is used in this book. Revelation 5:6 says that in heaven "stood a lamb as it had been slain…" When John the Baptist first saw Jesus, he proclaimed, "behold the Lamb of God which taketh away the sin of the world!" (John 1:29). The Lamb refers to Christ in his great work as the sacrifice. His sacrificial work not only paid the price for your redemption and mine but for the whole creation as well. The title of "The Lamb" refers to Christ's sacrificial work.

When that spectacular new age of the third heaven and earth comes to pass, the one who made it all possible will be our Lord Jesus Christ who laid down his life as an offering. Jesus Christ is not just "our" approach offering, but he is **the** approach offering for all eternity. We may sing a new song at the gates of the heavenly city, but it will be the old old story we have loved so long.

Notes

1. Craig Koester, *The Anchor Bible, Hebrews*, (New York: Doubleday, 2001), 334.

2. David J. Williams, *Paul's Metaphors* (Peabody: Mass.: Hendrickson, 1999), 205.

3. *Young's Concordance* defines Mt. Zion as "the S.W. hill of Jerusalem, the older and higher part of the city; it is also called the city of David" (page 1089). On this location Solomon later constructed the temple.

4. Leviticus 10:1-3. Another instance, which took place eight centuries later, is recorded in II Chronicles 26:16ff. King Uzziah wrongly approached the altar of incense in the temple to burn incense in spite of being withstood by the priests—"fourscore priests of the Lord, that were valiant men." The king was instantly afflicted with leprosy. The Way was NOT yet open.

5. Bullinger, *Figures of Speech used in the Bible*, page 521: under *Heterosis* of the tense: "The present for the future: this is put when the design is to show that some thing will certainly come to pass, and is spoken of as though it were already present." Also see II Peter 3:11,12. In Ephesians 2 the believer is "seat**ed**" and in Romans 8 the believer is "glorif**ied**"—a future certainty is in the past tense. The emphasis of this figure is on the certainty; in God's determination it is regarded as already accomplished. This is a fine example of a figure being "truer to truth"— more vivid and more real than the literal statement itself.

6. Ceslas Spicq, *Lexicon*, Volume III, page 6. The Greek writer, Isocrates, said, "I am often amazed that the founders of *panēguris* and the organizers of gymnastic competitions should think physical advantage to be worthy of such great rewards." In other words, he complained about the high salaries of top athletes. Remarkably, the same complaint is made today. Another writer said in a more spiritual vein, "Work to be crowned. . .with a noble and glorious crown that no *panēguris* among humankind offers."

7. Ceslas Spicq, *Lexicon*, Volume III, 6.

8. "The" is omitted in the Greek text. If it read "**the** firstborn" it would point to Christ. As it reads in the text it refers to the Church. Robertson, V, 440.

9. See Leviticus 27:26, Exodus 34:19 and Numbers 18:15-17 where it establishes that the "firstborn" are the redeemed. This prominent, but little known, Old Testament truth is covered in my three articles entitled, "The Great Levitical Swap." (***The Far View***, June 2000 through January 2001). Also see: Pink, *Hebrews*, 1052.

10. Koester, 545.

11. Category 5 in *Walking in God's Power,*® *intermediate class, Student Study Guide.*

12. Revelation 21:9,14, 22, 23, 27 and 22:1,3.

Appendix A

Boldness: Our Privilege as Citizens of Heaven

In looking at the historical background of the usage of the Greek word *parrhēsia,* one uncovers some great truths. The word boldness is from the Greek word *parrhēsia*, meaning freedom of speech, candor; plainness of speech; outspokenness; absence of fear in speaking. The French Bible scholar, Ceslas Spicq, states that in the Greek literature, the first meaning of *parrhēsia* is political: "the right to make one's thoughts known, to say what one will. It is a citizen's privilege, the sign of his political liberty, characterizing the democratic regime of the *polis* [city]. The citizen has the right to express his opinions freely."[1]

This understanding of *parrhēsia* is quite remarkable in light of our being called citizens of heaven in Philippians.

> Philippians 3:20:
> For our conversation [citizenship, *politeuma*] is in heaven; from whence also we look [*apekdechomi*, with body and head stretched forth eagerly waiting to receive] for the Saviour, the Lord Jesus Christ.

Ephesians sets forth the doctrine of our heavenly blessings, heavenly inheritance and heavenly seating. Here in Philippians more instruction is given to remedy the practical failure to apply this truth. In both Philippians 1:27 and 3:20 the word "conversation" is the Greek word *politeuma*, meaning "citizenship." This word comes from the word *polis*, meaning "city state."

The city of Philippi had a unique standing in the Roman Empire: it was recognized as an "Imperial city". Many of the residents of Philippi were Roman citizens, though detached from Rome. They enjoyed the same rights and privileges as if their land were part of Italian soil.[2] In reality, Philippi was far from Rome on the distant eastern shore of Macedonia (northern Greece). God, by revelation to Paul, drew a graphic picture of the exalted privilege of heavenly citizenship by drawing a parallel to the freedoms they enjoyed as "Romans" living in Philippi.

Although we reside here on earth, our citizenship is in heaven. As citizens of heaven we have all the rights, privileges and responsibilities that citizenship entitles. Although being absent from our home, as citizens of God's *polis,* we should set our affections, our aspirations and our hope on things above. Our allegiance and our source of guidance are from heaven. We should conduct ourselves as legal residents of heaven since that will be our ultimate destination. We are a heavenly people with a heavenly origin and heavenly destination. We have an accessible heavenly Father by way of our Lord Jesus Christ who is set at God's right hand in the heavenlies. We have been blessed with all spiritual blessings and have been legally seated in the heavenlies. Our heavenly citizenship gives us heavenly rights, privileges and responsibilities. One of those great heavenly privileges is our freedom of speech before God! So, let's approach our heavenly Father with freedom of speech, with candor, opening our hearts to Him.

Notes

1. Ceslas Spicq, *Lexicon*, III, 56.
2. *The New Bible Dictionary*, Eerdmans, 985.

Appendix B

The Peace Offering:
A Double Demonstration of Christ's Identification with His People

The New Testament exhorts us to look at the Old Testament sacrifices.

> I Corinthians 10:18:
> Behold Israel after the flesh: are not they which eat of the sacrifices partakers of the altar?

"Behold Israel after the flesh. . ." The verb for "behold" in the Greek is in the imperative, meaning a command. God commands us to look at how those, "...which eat of the sacrifices" are "partakers of the altar."

To carry out this command to the Body of Christ in the Church Epistles, we must look at this topic of sacrifices where it has been used before in the Scriptures. The sacrifices, which "Israel after the flesh," ate, are not explained in Corinthians. For that matter, they are not clarified anywhere else in New Testament. In order for us to "behold Israel" and the sacrifices they consumed, we will have to go to the Mosaic Law where these sacrifices were instituted and described. We will need to check where this topic of sacrifice has been explained and "used before."

Appendix B: The Peace Offering

When God in His Word requires one to remember what was explained previously, one often becomes confused, and says, "What does the Bible mean? Why isn't this explained better? Is the Bible deliberately obscure or was it just written too long ago?" Some seem to blame God or the Scriptures for appearing so ambiguous. In truth, such an attitude holds God and His Word to a standard not imposed on secular writers.

For example, suppose you are reading the exciting closing pages of a thousand-page Tom Clancy novel. The suspense is running high. How will it turn out? Will the bad guy get away? How will the good guy survive? Now in these exciting closing pages will the novelist pause and take three pages to re-explain something he has already covered? No, you, the reader, are supposed to remember what was explained 900 pages ago. You are supposed to recall the various pieces of data from the book. In the closing, in the climax, it all comes together. A secular author does not insult his reader's intelligence by laboring over a re-explanation of what he has already spelled out earlier. Likewise, in the Scriptures, God will often not re-explain what He has spelled out before.

I Corinthians 10:18 prompts us to refer back to the sacrificial system of Israel. Over a thousand pages earlier in the Bible, in Leviticus, the offerings are instituted and explained in detail.

Most would look at I Corinthians 10:18 and assume it is referring to Old Testament offerings in general. But this verse is only referring to offerings that are <u>eaten</u>. This fact narrows down the field considerably. The burnt offering was completely consumed on the altar. No part of it was eaten. The meal offering was partially consumed on the altar while the priests ate the remainder. With the sin and

trespass offerings, the fat was consumed on the altar while the remainder of the carcass was burned outside the camp.
The peace offering was the only sacrifice of the five whereby a portion is returned to the offerer to eat.

The exhortation of I Corinthians 10:18 to examine this Old Testament offering is not an easy one for Bible students of today. Animal sacrifice is almost unheard of in our modern world. Our eyes glaze over when we read sections of the Mosaic Law about sacrifices and offerings. In reading about the various sacrifices and various steps, the details can mix together into an seemingly incomprehensible muddle. It is difficult for us to relate to animal sacrifices, much less grasp the meaning behind those activities. While the significance of sacrifices is an enigma to us, in the lands and times of the Bible, animal sacrifices were an integral and vital part of the culture and were universally understood.

These sacrifices dramatically foreshadow the coming Messiah. But our understanding is obscured unless we perceive their function and meaning in the ancient world. As we take time to examine these sacrifices, we will acquire a stronger grasp of what Christ has accomplished for us.

The Peace Offering

Like the burnt offering and meal offering, the peace offering was a "sweet savour" offering unto the Lord. In contrast to the sin and the trespass offerings, the main emphasis was on offering a sweet fragrance unto the Lord, not on the sin or cleansing of the offerer. But, unlike the burnt, meal, sin, and trespass offering, with the peace offering the offerer was allowed to eat of the offering.

Three Portions of the Peace Offering

While most of the peace offering was eaten by the offerer, it was divided up in three portions according to the Law.

1. The Lord's Portion: Leviticus three

Leviticus chapter three is not a full explanation of the peace offering. This chapter only addresses the Lord's portion of the peace offering—the fat of the sacrifice. Leviticus three does not explain what portion the priest received or what the offerer received. Instead, this chapter only details the portion that the Lord was to receive—the fat of the animal. The chapter is summed up by Leviticus 3:16: ". . .all the fat is the Lord's." This truth, that all the fat of a sacrifice belonged to the Lord and was to be burned on the altar, became an established principle that continued throughout Scripture. Even the fat of the sin offering was to be burned on the altar. (Leviticus 4:8-10, 19, 26, 31, 35).

The sons of Eli, in I Samuel 2, disregarded this command of God that all fat was to be burned unto the Lord. These "sons of Belial," as they were also called, committed a gross violation of this sacred principle of sacrifice by keeping the fat for themselves. They caused the people to "abhor the offering of the Lord."

In the ancient world, the fat of an animal was considered the most desirable part of the animal. In our society we eat too much fat and the wrong kind. However fat still adds desirability and flavor to foods. Imagine the taste of a cheeseburger, fries and a milk shake devoid of any fat. Without the fat, the meal would be fairly tasteless.

The fat was the best and the choicest portion. This portion was burned as incense on the altar unto the Lord. Truly, this portion of the offering points to Christ. The best, "the choice," of all humanity was the Lord Jesus Christ. He offered himself on our behalf. He was the very best God had to offer.

2. The Priest's Portion: Leviticus 7:29-34:

> Speak unto the children of Israel, saying, He that offereth the sacrifice of his peace offerings unto the LORD shall bring his oblation unto the LORD of the sacrifice of his peace offerings.
> His own hands shall bring the offerings of the LORD made by fire, the fat with the breast, it shall he bring, that the breast may be waved *for* a wave offering before the LORD.
> And the priest shall burn the fat upon the altar [the Lord's portion]: but **the breast shall be Aaron's and his sons'.**
> And **the right shoulder shall ye give unto the priest** *for* an heave offering of the sacrifices of your peace offerings.
> He among the sons of Aaron, that offereth the blood of the peace offerings, and the fat, shall have the right shoulder for *his* part.

> For the **wave breast and the heave shoulder have I taken of the children of Israel from off the sacrifices of their peace offerings, and have given them unto Aaron the priest and unto his sons** by a statute for ever from among the children of Israel.

The priest's portion of the peace offering was the breast and the right shoulder of the animal. These were given to the priests to eat. The "wave breast and the heave shoulder" meant that these portions have been transferred to God and now belonged to Him. Then the priests could eat them. (Waving and heaving have similar meanings, signifying a change of ownership. Once the breast was waved and the shoulder was heaved, these portions legally belonged to God and were the priest's to eat.)[1]

3. The Offerer's Portion   Leviticus 7:11-27

The fat was removed from the animal and burned on the altar as the Lord's portion. The priest received the breast and the right shoulder of the animal as his portion. Then the remainder of the animal was given back to the offerer. At that point he and his family and friends could eat what was left of the peace offering.

> Leviticus 19:5,6:
> And if ye offer a sacrifice of peace offerings unto the LORD, ye shall offer it at your own will.
> It shall be eaten the same day ye offer it, and on the morrow: and if ought remain until the third day, it shall be burnt in the fire.

The peace offering was to be eaten by the offerer.

> Deuteronomy 27:7:
> And thou shalt offer peace offerings, and shalt eat there, and rejoice before the LORD thy God.

Sharing a fellowship meal around the peace offerings was to be a time of joy. Such a mutual partaking foreshadowed the coming Messiah who would share fully with his people by his sacrifice.

Three Varieties of the Peace Offering

Three kinds of peace offerings are set forth in Leviticus 7:11-36. Each has a different function.

1. The thanksgiving offering was to praise or thank God for His blessings.

> Leviticus 7:12-15:
> If he offer it for a thanksgiving, then he shall offer with the sacrifice of thanksgiving unleavened cakes mingled with oil, and unleavened wafers anointed with oil, and cakes mingled with oil, of fine flour, fried.
> Besides the cakes, he shall offer *for* his offering leavened bread with the sacrifice of thanksgiving of his peace offerings.
> And of it he shall offer one out of the whole oblation *for* an heave offering unto the LORD, *and* it shall be the priest's that sprinkleth the blood of the peace offerings.
> And the flesh of the sacrifice of his peace offerings for thanksgiving shall be eaten the same day that it is offered; he shall not leave any of it until the morning.

2. The vow offering, *neder* in Hebrew, was brought following the successful fulfillment of a vow. (Also see: I Samuel 1:21, Proverbs 7:14).

> Leviticus 7:16:
> But if the sacrifice of his offering *be* a **vow** [*neder*], or a voluntary [freewill, *nedabah*] offering, it shall be eaten the same day that he offereth his sacrifice: and on the morrow also the remainder of it shall be eaten:

> Leviticus 22:21:
> And whosoever offereth a sacrifice of peace offerings unto the LORD to accomplish *his* vow [*neder*], or a freewill [*nedabah*] offering in beeves or sheep, it shall be perfect to be accepted; there shall be no blemish therein.

> Numbers 15:8:
> And when thou preparest a bullock *for* a burnt offering, or *for* a sacrifice in performing a vow [*neder*], or peace offerings unto the LORD:

3. The voluntary or freewill [*nedabah*] offering was given freely, spontaneously, with a willing mind.[2] As the above verses (Leviticus 7:16, 22:21) show, this offering was often paired with the vow offering. The freewill offering was not limited to a peace offering but could also be gifts or money (Exodus 35:29, Ezra 8:28).

The Significance of the Eating the Peace Offering

As we have seen, the unique characteristic of the peace offering was that a major part of the offering was given back to the offerer to eat. The offerer partook of the offering. Since the meat would spoil quickly and the animal was more than one person could eat, the peace offering usually involved a sacrificial meal. The family and friends of the offerer would be invited to partake of the peace offering together. They fellowshipped together, in communion with each other as they ate the offering. Andrew Jukes in *The Law of the Offerings* says of the peace offering:

> . . .*In it the offerer, the priest, and God, all fed together*. This was the case in no other offering but the Peace-offering. In this they had something in common. Here each had a part. They held communion in feeding on the same offering.[3]

Eating of the sacrifice together represented a full sharing with the sacrifice and with each other. The NIV calls the peace offering the "fellowship offering."

This understanding brings us to a most critical question: What did eating a sacrifice signify? The second phrase of I Corinthians 10:18 informs us of exactly what eating a sacrifice meant:

> I Corinthians 10:18:
> Behold Israel after the flesh: are not **they which eat of the sacrifices partakers [*koinōnos*] of the altar?**

Koinōnos is a form of *koinōnia,* meaning to "share fully." The second phase of this verse is a rhetorical question: ". . .are not they which eat of the sacrifices partakers [*koinōnos*] of the altar?" Yes indeed, those who ate sacrifices did share fully with the altar. The altar represented the sacrifices offered on it. Those who ate of the sacrifices shared fully with those sacrifices. To eat that sacrifice was to have a spiritual union with that sacrifice. The intent in eating a sacrifice was to identify, to fully share with what that sacrifice represented. As I Corinthians 10:18 says, "they which eat of the sacrifices" share fully; that was the significance of eating a sacrifice.

As Old Testament believers ingested that sacrifice, what it represented was transferred to them. The same essence of that offering was ingested into their being. Hence, they became "identified" with that sacrifice. What that sacrifice represented resided in them, and they resided in it. In a sense, whatever that sacrifice was, they became. That is what eating a sacrifice meant in Bible times.[4] In the same way, we share fully in Christ's sacrifice under the New Covenant.

Peace Offering: Double Demonstration of Identification

In addition to what we have just seen, the peace offering held one more demonstration of identification with the offerer.

> Leviticus 3:1,2, 8, 13:
> And if his oblation [offering] *be* a sacrifice of **peace offering**, if he offer *it* of the herd; whether *it be* a male or female, he shall offer it without blemish before the Lord.
> And he shall **lay his hand upon the head** of his offering . . .
> And he shall **lay his hand upon the head** of his offering and kill it before the tabernacle. . .
> And he shall **lay his hand upon the head** of it, and kill it before the tabernacle. . .

In these verses, identification is symbolized by laying the hand of the offerer on the sacrifice. This physical contact signified a transfer—all the unworthiness and sin of the man was transferred to the animal, and all the innocence and acceptableness of the offering was transferred to the offerer. This laying on of the hand also takes place with the burnt offering and the sin offering.

There are two great demonstrations of identification in the Old Testament sacrificial system:[5]
    1. Laying a hand on the head of the sacrifice.
    2. Eating the sacrifice.
Only with the peace offering, are these two elements brought together in one offering.

With regard to the Passover lamb and the peace offering, the eating of the sacrifice demonstrates that identification— that full sharing with that sacrifice. However, with the peace offering the offerer laid a hand on the offering **and** ate the sacrifice. The great lesson of the peace offering is that it foreshadows our full sharing with the future, *true* sacrifice of Jesus Christ. Thus, the peace offering sets forth a spectacular two-fold illustration of our identification with Christ.

Peace Offering: Parallel to Christ

As we have seen, the peace offering prefigures our identification with Christ. This offering served as an illustration of the full sharing the believers would have with the coming Messiah. Just as the Old Covenant believers ingested the peace offering, so those of the New Covenant would ingest Christ. The peace offering symbolizes our identification with Christ. This offering foreshadows the utter oneness and full union we would have with Christ. He dwells in us and we in him.

In the Old Testament, the offerers were filled with the flesh of the peace offering. We are filled with all the fullness of God in Christ. While this offering was a mere flickering shadow of that which was to come, what a lesson it has to teach of Christ! In its faint light, we can see the glorious work of Christ accomplished in every believer. We share fully with him! When he died, we died with him. When he arose, we arose with him. We can now walk in the newness of resurrection life.

The dominant and most arresting characteristic of the peace offering was the double demonstration of the full sharing of the offerer and the sacrifice. The offerer laid his hand on the head of the sacrifice and then consumed the sacrifice. This was two separate acts, but only one great truth—identification with the sacrifice. The peace offering represented that which was to come: the spiritual ingestion of all that Christ is unto every believer.

He is our Peace Offering

> Ephesians 2:13-16:
> But now in Christ Jesus ye who sometimes were far off are made nigh [near] by the blood of Christ.
> For **he is our peace**, who hath made both one, and hath broken down the middle wall of partition *between us*;
> Having abolished in his flesh the enmity, *even* the law of commandments *contained* in ordinances; for to make in himself of twain one new man, *so* making peace;
> And that he might reconcile both unto God in one body by the cross, having slain the enmity thereby:

Some have suggested that a word should be supplied after "peace" in verse 14. The word "maker" or "treaty" has been suggested. "For he is our peace treaty. . ." would tie in with the mention of "enmity" in verse 15 and 16. A peace treaty brings two warring parties together. However, a peace treaty, while it dissolves enmity, does not "make both one." A peace treaty usually does not entail a merger; rather it indicates an end of hostilities. A peace treaty does not make of two "one new man, so making peace." (Verse 15).

The context of verse 14 is that of sacrifice. Verse 13 mentions the blood of Christ given in sacrifice. Verse 15 references the accomplishments of the flesh of Christ given in sacrifice. To supply the word "offering" right after "peace" would better fit with this context.

The idea of a peace offering also fits well with the following phrase: "who hath made **both one**." As we have seen, the one sacrifice that the people ate together was the peace offering. This offering indicated a full sharing and communion in the fellowship meal. God, the priest and offerers all shared of one sacrifice. The fat was burned on the altar to God. The priest got the right shoulder and the breast. The offerer got the remainder. The thought was that of spiritual union and fellowship between all parties. The role of the peace offering was to bring them all together.

In Ephesians 2:13-16 the offering of Christ brings together God and His people: "made nigh. . .the both one. . .broken down wall. . .of twain one new man. . .reconcile both unto God **by the cross**. . ." Intertwining through these verses is the full sharing and reconciliation of God's people accomplished by Christ's perfect sacrifice.

The idea of spiritual communion and full sharing is also the context of the reference to the peace offering in I Corinthians 10:18.

I Corinthians 10:16-18:
The cup of blessing which we bless, is it not the communion of the blood of Christ? The bread which we break, is it not the communion of the body [flesh of Christ given in sacrifice] of Christ?
For we *being* many are one bread, *and* one body [of the church]: for we are all partakers of that one bread.
Behold Israel after the flesh: are not they which eat of the sacrifices [peace offerings] partakers of the altar?

Verse 17 says: "we *being* many are one," and we are "one body," and "we are all partakers." As with Ephesians 2:14-17, the big point here is oneness.

In Ephesians 2, as in I Corinthians 10, the role of the Old Testament peace offering is alluded to. Although not mentioned by name, it is implied. What a touching picture the peace offering gives us! We envision a group of Old Covenant believers sitting down and feasting on the peace offering in fellowship together. What we feast on in the New Covenant is much richer and more glorious. We share fully in the riches of His grace.

Notes

1. David Bergey, *The Far View,* "The Wave Offering: A Shadow of Things to Come"(November 2000).

2. Gesenius', *Lexicon*, 534.

3. Jukes, *The Law of the Offerings*, 99.

4. My publication, *Our Identification with Christ's Sacrifice,* has an appendix that documents from sources outside the Scriptures that eating food sacrificed to an idol indicates an identification and sharing with that idol. This was precisely the issue in I Corinthians 10:19-31.

> I Corinthians 10:18-21:
> Behold Israel after the flesh: are not they which eat of the sacrifices partakers [*koinōnos*] of the altar?
> What say I then? that the idol is any thing, or that which is offered in sacrifice to idols is any thing?
> But I *say*, that the things which the Gentiles sacrifice, they sacrifice to devils, and not to God: and I would not that ye should have fellowship [*koinonia*] with devils.
> Ye cannot drink the cup of the Lord, and the cup of devils: ye cannot be partakers [*metecho*, full participants] of the Lord's table, and of the table of devils.

Here the Apostle Paul explains exactly what occurs when the Gentiles sacrifice to their idols. These sacrifices they offer are to devil spirits represented by the idols. Also, eating and drinking these sacrifices offered to devil spirits symbolizes a full sharing [*koinonia*]. The intent of eating and drinking these sacrifices was to identify, to share with idols, or—as the Apostle candidly says—devils. This admonishment goes back to a common understanding in ancient times: When you eat food sacrificed and dedicated to an idol, you are spiritually identifying and sharing with that idol.

5. David Bergey, *Our Identification with Christ's Sacrifice*, 20-37. The topic of identification and how it relates to Old Testament sacrifices is explained in this publication.

Subject Index

Aaron, 32, 35, 79, 84, 121, 123, 137, 138, 140, 141, 148, 150, 176, 177, 178, 196, 197
Abel, 178, 182
Abraham, 71, 91, 108, 109, 111, 157
abundant sharing, 15
access is influence, 9
Adam, 13, 32, 75, 98, 99, 102, 175, 176, 185
amōmos, 119, 120, 124, 133, 159, 163, 164
anchor, 170, 171, 173
anegkletous, 162
anointed; anointing, 105, 148, 149, 150, 153, 198
Antithesis, 90, 91
ascent, 35, 81, 174
bears witness, 102, 103, 104, 166
burn incense, 43, 44, 51, 52, 188
burnt offering, 21, 34
Cain, 182, 183
Christ's flesh, 82, 83, 84, 90
Church Epistles, 125, 192
citizenship, 181, 190, 191
holy communion, 15, 19, 82, 200
corban, 35
Cornelius, 104, 145
cornerstone, 60, 75
courts, 9, 10, 27
covenant making, 85, 86, 87, 182
cowered in fear, 102
curse of the Law, 57
Daniel, 67
Day of Atonement, 32, 79, 80, 126, 127, 131, 140
Day of Pentecost, 49, 61, 104, 151
definite article, 96, 115, 132, 164
deisidaimon, 100
door (Christ), 71
dread in approaching, 101
echō, 93, 94, 95
Epaphras, 110, 111
Esther, 9, 10
face-to-face, 99, 101, 102, 151, 155, 156, 157, 158, 163, 165, 166, 178
Fall of Man, 74, 99, 176
fat, 44, 137, 194, 195, 196, 197, 204
figures of speech, 29, 35, 42, 91
firstborn, 177, 178, 180, 189

flesh of Christ, 57, 82, 83, 84, 86, 89, 90, 204, 205
forerunner, 170, 174
freewill offering, 122, 199
fruit of the spirit, 103, 151
full assurance, 64, 70, 93, 97, 107, 108, 112, 113, 126, 128, 172, 173, 174
Gathering Together, 164, 165, 170, 174, 179, 184
genitive of origin, 108, 117, 145
God's evaluation, 119
Golgotha, 4
grace, 54, 65, 67, 81, 98, 113, 143, 151, 162, 205
grieving process, 172
hagiazo, 144, 145
hagios, 133, 134, 142, 144, 145
healing, 149, 151
hearts sprinkled, 64, 70, 93, 107, 126, 127
heave offering, 86, 196, 197, 198
heavenly Jerusalem, 68, 177, 178, 179, 181, 182, 184
heifer, 125, 132
Heterosis, 179, 188
high priest, 8, 32, 54, 58, 61, 63, 64, 69, 77, 79, 80, 81, 84, 87, 93, 126, 127, 131, 170, 174, 176, 177, 182
holy of holies, 8, 27, 59, 60, 64, 78, 79, 80, 81, 84, 126, 127
identification, 124, 125, 201, 202, 203, 206, 207
illegitimate approach, 32, 140
inner man, 127, 128
intercession, 62, 69, 81, 89, 104
katenopion, 155, 157, 158, 162
katharizō, 126, 147
koinōnia, 200
Korah, 141, 142, 178
Lamb, (Christ) 45, 124, 180, 186
Lucifer, 185
manifestation of the spirit, 58, 103, 112, 150, 151
meal offering, 21, 39, 42, 43, 51, 82, 193, 195
meat offering, 21
mediator, 54, 81, 178, 182
Melchisedec, 170, 177
Metalepsis or Double Metonymy, 167
metonymy, 159, 160, 161
middle wall of partition, 56, 57, 203
mode of entrée, 97

Moses, 7, 24, 42, 50, 57, 60, 66, 77, 78, 101, 121, 123, 137, 138, 140, 141, 176, 177, 178
Mount Sinai, 35, 42, 68, 101, 142, 176-178
Mount Zion, 68, 101, 176, 188
Nadab and Abihu, 35, 138
nedabah, 199
neder, 199
New Covenant, 23, 33, 46, 47, 49, 67, 83, 84, 122, 127, 134, 142, 148, 154, 202, 205
nullifying of the Law, 57
Old Covenant, 7, 16, 20, 21, 23, 26, 27, 29, 31, 38, 46, 49, 50, 55, 57, 61, 62, 68, 80, 123, 126, 127, 129, 133, 142, 157, 176, 178, 202, 205
Old Testament sacrifices, 12-27, 50, 55, 64-66, 86, 87, 121, 192, 207
panēguris, 179, 180, 189
paroimia, 76
parrhēsia, 2, 93, 95, 96, 98, 105, 106, 107, 110, 111, 113, 114, 190
peace offering, 21, 34, 40, 42, 44, 59, 161, 194, 195, 197, 198, 199, 200, 201, 202, 203, 204, 205
perfect indicative tense, 18
perfect praise, 49
perfect tense, 18, 128
Persian court etiquette, 10
plēroō, 5, 6
plērophoria, 107, 108, 110, 112
polyptoton, 28, 30, 31, 32, 35, 37, 38, 40, 41, 51
prayer, 11, 16, 37, 45, 46, 47, 50, 95, 107, 110, 111, 113, 114, 129, 150
prodromos, 170
prosagō, 55, 75, 172
prosagōgē, 54, 55, 58, 65, 75, 171, 172
proserkomai, 68, 69, 70, 76, 177, 178
prosphatos, 82
purification offering, 21
qadesh, 136, 137, 138, 140, 150
qadosh, 135, 136, 141
qarab, 25, 26, 28, 30, 31, 33, 34, 35, 37, 38, 39, 40, 41, 44, 45, 51, 56, 86, 121, 122, 123, 141
qatar, 33, 37, 43, 44, 45, 51, 52
qorban, 25, 26, 28, 30, 31, 34, 35, 38, 39, 40, 41, 44, 51, 53, 55, 86, 87, 121

renewing the mind, 98, 100, 146, 147
resurrection, 1, 61, 81, 82, 175, 181, 203
sabasma, 100, 116
salt covenant, 86
sanctification, 128, 134, 137, 144, 145, 146, 148, 152, 154
Septuagint, 55
silhouette, 12, 46
sin offering, 14, 21, 23, 42, 125, 126, 127, 129, 131, 137, 195, 202
sonship, 61, 102, 103, 165, 166
speaking in tongues, 47, 48, 49, 50, 104, 145, 151, 160
sprinkling, 36, 89, 125, 127, 128, 129, 131, 132, 148, 178, 182
substitution, 55, 65
sweet savour, 15, 21, 23, 34, 40, 44, 46, 195
tabernacle, 8, 24, 26, 27, 60, 61, 64, 66, 77, 78, 79, 80, 87, 123, 133, 137, 139, 140, 150, 176, 184, 185, 201
teleioō, 5, 6, 7
teleō, 5, 6, 18
temple, 14, 26, 27, 59, 60, 61, 75, 77, 78, 83, 84, 89, 92, 146, 188

temporary access, 13
thanksgiving offering, 198
The Way (Christ), 7, 8, 16, 24, 32, 50, 73, 74, 80, 81, 83, 84, 97, 178, 188
throne of grace, 8, 66, 67, 98, 143
throne room, 8, 10, 11, 27, 54, 58, 63, 94, 107
trespass offering, 13, 21, 41, 42, 44, 131, 194, 195
types, 7, 50, 90, 178
Uzziah, 188
vow offering, 199
wave, 196, 197
witness of the spirit, 103, 107

Scripture Index

GENESIS

Genesis 1:27. 98
Genesis 1:28-31. 98
Genesis 2:7. 174
Genesis 2:17. . . . . .31, 35
Genesis 3:8. . . . . . .98, 99
Genesis 4 182
Genesis 4:10 and 11...183
Genesis 4:14, 16. 183
Genesis 14:18. 177
Genesis 15:17, 18a. . . .85
Genesis 18:22. 157

EXODUS

Exodus 19 and 20. . . .101
Exodus 20:19. 101
Exodus 24:8-11. 36
Exodus 28:41. 150
Exodus 29:21. 148
Exodus 34:19. 189
Exodus 35:29. 200

LEVITICUS

Leviticus, chapter 1-7. . .
  20, 21, 24, 30, 33, 35,
  42, 51
Leviticus 1:1, 2. . . .24, 42
Leviticus 1:2 . . . . 25, 28,
  30, 31, 38
Leviticus 1:3. 39,121
Leviticus 1:9. 43
Leviticus 1:10. 39
Leviticus 1:13. . . . .34, 43
Leviticus 1:14. 39
Leviticus 1:15. . . . .39, 43
Leviticus 1:17. . . . .34, 43
Leviticus 2:1. 39
Leviticus 2:2. . . . . .34, 43
Leviticus 2:4. 39
Leviticus 2:9. . . . . .34, 43
Leviticus 2:11. 43
Leviticus 2:12. 40
Leviticus 2:13. . . . .40, 86
Leviticus 2:16. 43
Leviticus 3. 161,196
Leviticus 3:1. . . . .40, 201
Leviticus 3:2. 201
Leviticus 3:5. 44
Leviticus 3:6. 40
Leviticus 3:7. . . . . .40, 41
Leviticus 3:8. 201
Leviticus 3:11. 44
Leviticus 3:12. . . . .41, 52
Leviticus 3:13. 201
Leviticus 3:14. 41
Leviticus 3:16. 44
Leviticus 4:6. 89
Leviticus 4:8-10 ...19, 26,
  31, 35, 195
Leviticus 4:10. 44
Leviticus 4:17. 89
Leviticus 4:19. 44

Leviticus 4: 21....... 52
Leviticus 6:9......... .52
Leviticus 6:12......... .52
Leviticus 6:13......... .52
Leviticus 7:11-36.... .161
Leviticus 7:11-27.... .198
Leviticus 7:11-36.... .199
Leviticus 7:12-15.... .199
Leviticus 7:13....... 41
Leviticus 7:14....... 41
Leviticus 7:16 .. .41, 56, 200
Leviticus 7:29....... .41
Leviticus 7:29-34.... .197
Leviticus 7:37, 38..... .42
Leviticus 8:12....... .149
Leviticus 9:22-24.... .137
Leviticus 10:1-3.... .138, 188
Leviticus 11:44,45... .136
Leviticus 14:6, 7.... .131
Leviticus 15:31..... .139
Leviticus 16......... .80
Leviticus 16:1-3..... .140
Leviticus 16:4....... .131
Leviticus 16:19...... .131
Leviticus 19:2....... .136
Leviticus 19:5,6..... .198
Leviticus 20:24-26... .135
Leviticus 21:16-23... .123
Leviticus 22:9....... .140
Leviticus 22:17-25... .121
Leviticus 22:21...... .200
Leviticus 22:32, 33... .136
Leviticus 27:26...... .189

NUMBERS

Numbers 15:8....... .200
Numbers 16:1-5..... .141
Numbers 16:27-33... .178
Numbers 18:15-17... .189
Numbers 18:19....... .86
Numbers 28......... .82

DEUTERONOMY

Deuteronomy 7:6.... .135
Deuteronomy 14:2... .135
Deuteronomy 14:3-21, 135
Deuteronomy 21:17.. .180
Deuteronomy 27:7... .199

SAMUEL

I Samuel 1:21....... .200
I Samuel 2......... .196

KINGS

I Kings 8:38 and 39.. .19
I Kings 9:11-13...... .18

CHRONICLES

I Chronicles 23-26... .14
II Chronicles 20:8, 9... 19
II Chronicles 26:16... 188

EZRA

Ezra 8:28..........200

ESTHER

Esther 1:14...........9
Esther 4:11...........9

PSALMS

Psalm 18:6-16........19
Psalm 20:2...........19
Psalm 40:6...........14
Psalm 62:8...........97
Psalm 65:4...........26
Psalm 100:4..........27
Psalm 102:1,2,18,19...19
Psalm 141:2......... 45

PROVERBS

Proverbs 7:14.......200

ISAIAH

Isaiah 28:16..........75
Isaiah 53......13, 90, 131
Isaiah 53:10..........13

JEREMIAH

Jeremiah 15:16.......112
Jeremiah 34:18...... 85

DANIEL

Daniel 3:16-18........67
Daniel 3:27...........67

JONAH

Jonah 2:4-7..........19

MATTHEW

Matthew 5:17.........89
Matthew 21:22.......113
Matthew 26:53.........3
Matthew 27:50, 51... 78
Matthew 27:51........83

MARK

Mark 16:17..........104
Mark 7:11............35

LUKE

Luke 1:19...........155
Luke 4:7 and 8......156
Luke 16:24...........75
Luke 22:42............4
Luke 23:45...........78

JOHN

John 1:29...........186
John 1:46............18
John 3:16...........160
John 4:24............98

John 7:41, 52. 18
John 10:1, 2, 9. 76
John 10:1-17 71
John 10:9. 76
John 14:3. 174
John 14:6. . . . . . . .7, 73
John 19:16-30. 4
John 19:28. 6

ACTS

Acts 2:1-4. 49
Acts 2:4. . . . . 49, 104
Acts 2:25. 156
Acts 10. . .104, 145, 149
Acts 10:28. 145
Acts 10:46. 145
Acts 17:22 and 23. . .100
Acts 27:29 and 30. . .171

ROMANS

Romans 1:14-16. 62
Romans 4:20 and 21...108
Romans 4:21. . . .71, 108
Romans 5:2. . .54, 70, 75, 171, 172
Romans 5:2-8. 65
Romans 5:9-11. 66
Romans 6:6. 124
Romans 8. . . . . . .64, 188
Romans 8:15. 103
Romans 8:15-18 . . .102, 165
Romans 8:16. . .103, 104, 116
Romans 8:17. . . .102,181
Romans 8:22. 185
Romans 8:31-39 62
Romans 8:34. 69
Romans 8:37-39 64
Romans 10:17. 111
Romans 10:9. 145
Romans 15:16. 145

I CORINTHIANS

I Corinthians 1:30. . .137
I Corinthians 10:16-18. . . 206
I Corinthians 10:18. . . 193, 194, 201
I Corinthians 10:18-21. . . 207
I Corinthians 11. 15
I Corinthians 12:7-10. . . . 58, 150
I Corinthians 13:9-12. . . . 164
I Corinthians 14. 47
I Corinthians 14:14,15. . . 47
I Corinthians 14:16. . . 49
I Corinthians 14:16-19. . . 48
I Corinthians 14:22. . . . 104
I Corinthians 15:26...176
I Corinthians 15:35...175

I Corinthians 15:48-50......175
I Corinthians 15:51-55......175

II CORINTHIANS

II Corinthians 2:17...167
II Corinthians 3:12...95
II Corinthians 3:13...89
II Corinthians 4:13...94
II Corinthians 5:21...125
II Corinthians 6:16-7:1......146
II Corinthians 7:1...95, 146
II Corinthians 12:19......167

GALATIANS

Galatians 2:20......124
Galatians 5:22, 23......116,151

EPHESIANS

Ephesians 1:4.........119, ..120, 133, 137, 155, 158, 162
Ephesians 1:4,7......137
Ephesians 2......59,188, ..205
Ephesians 2:11-13....56
Ephesians 2:13-16...59, ..90, 204
Ephesians 2:13......59, ..90, 162, 204, 205
Ephesians 2:14...56, 59, ..162
Ephesians 2:15...56, 59
Ephesians 2:14-17....59, ..206
Ephesians 2:16...46, 58, ..59
Ephesians 2:17....58, 59
Ephesians 2:18...54, 58, ..59 107, 146, 151, 171
Ephesians 2:19-22....59
Ephesians 3:12...54, 96, ..118,171
Ephesians 4:2,15,16..167
Ephesians 3:17......167
Ephesians 5:2....23, 167
Ephesians 6:18......47

PHILIPPIANS

Philippians 1:27......191
Philippians 2:15......120
Philippians 3:18......160
Philippians 3:20......191
Philippians 3:20, 21...174
Philippians 4:3...143, 181
Philippians 4:18......15

COLOSSIANS

Colossians 1:7......110
Colossians 1:20......90, ..159,161,167

Colossians 1:20-22. . . 90, 159
Colossians 1:22. . . . .119, 143, 144, 162
Colossians 2:2. 167
Colossians 3:16. 111
Colossians 4:12, 13...110

THESSALONIANS

I Thessalonians 1:5...112
I Thessalonians 4:13-18... 169, 179, 184
I Thessalonians 5:17..117

II Thessalonians 2:13..145

TIMOTHY

II Timothy 1:7. 100
II Timothy 3:16. 162

TITUS

Titus 3:5 and 6. 129

PHILEMON

Philemon 23. 110

HEBREWS

Hebrews 4. . . . . . . .8, 98
Hebrews 4:16. . . . .68, 98
Hebrews 6:11, 12. . . .172

Hebrews 6:18. 173
Hebrews 6:18-20. . . . 170
Hebrews 6:20. 177
Hebrews 7:23-25. 69
Hebrews 7:25. . . .68, 69, 81, 182
Hebrews 9:1-3. 78
Hebrews 9:7 and 8. . . .79
Hebrews 9:13 . . .125,131
Hebrews 9:14. . . . . .124, 125, 131, 182
Hebrews 9:15. 182
Hebrews 9:21, 22. . . .131
Hebrews 9:28. . .23, 46, 55
Hebrews 10:1. . .13, 38, 46, 68
Hebrews 10:1-3. 12
Hebrews 10:10. 90
Hebrews 10:11, 12. . . .87
Hebrews 10:11-22. . . .92
Hebrews 10:14. 87
Hebrews 10:19. . . . 7, 74, 81, 82, 84, 85, 93, 94, 95, 97, 107, 126
Hebrews 10:20. . .74, 81, 82, 84, 85, 126
Hebrews 10:19-21. . .81
Hebrews 11:21. 75
Hebrews 10:19-22. . . 63, 64
Hebrews 10:22. . .63, 64, 68, 70, 90, 107, 108, 127, 128
Hebrews 10:32-34. . .110

Hebrews 10:34...110, 181
Hebrews 10:35, 36...110
Hebrews 11:6...68, 70, 109
Hebrews 11:35, 40...181
Hebrews 12:16......180
Hebrews 12:18......68, 101, 177
Hebrews 12:18-21...101
Hebrews 12:18-24...177
Hebrews 12:22......68, 178, 179, 184
Hebrews 12:23....178, 181
Hebrews 12:24....178, 182
Hebrews 13:12....48, 143, 144
Hebrews 13:12-16...48
Hebrews 13:14....179

PETER

I Peter 1:18 and 19...124
I Peter 1:2......128, 148
I Peter 3:18.........55
II Peter 3:11,12......188

I JOHN

I John 2:28........105
I John 3:1...........8
I John 3:19-22.....114
I John 4:13-18......106
I John 4:17.........106
I John 5:14...95, 106, 113
I John 5:15.........113

JUDE

Jude 1 and 2........163
Jude 24.........163, 171
Jude 24 and 25......164

REVELATION

Revelation 5:6......186
Revelation 5:8.......45
Revelation 8:2......156
Revelation 21.......179
Revelation 21, 22....184
Revelation 21:1-4....184
Revelation 21:2...... 186
Revelation 21:3.....184
Revelation 21:4...184,185
Revelation 21:9,14, 22, 23, 27...........189
Revelation 22:1,3....189
Revelation 22:14.....76

Jesus Christ Our Approach Offering
by
David Bergey

ORDER FORM

Name_____
Address_____
City, State, Zip _____
Country (if not USA)_____
Phone _____

Book Pricing:	1 copy:	$15.00
	2-9 copies	$12 per book
	10+	$ 10 per book

Shipping: $3.00 for the first book and $1.00 for each additional book within US, Canada and Mexico. International orders add $6.00 for first book and $2.00 for each additional book.

_____ Copies of book $_____

Postage and handling $_____

Total amount enclosed $_____

Make checks payable to **Redlands Bible Fellowship**
And mail to:

Redlands Bible Fellowship
1308 Farview Lane
Redlands, CA 92374
Fax: (909) 798-9660

Other Publications by the same author:
Our Identification with Christ's Sacrifice: $6.00 (postage included)
Isaac Newton: Workman of God's Word: $6.00 (postage included)